# All the King's Men

RANDALL J. BREWER

# ALL THE KING'S MEN

# CONTENTS

# INTRODUCTION

Every kingdom is only as strong as the men who serve within it. The same is true in the spiritual realm. The kingdom of God thrives not through passive belief, but through the bold, disciplined, and faithful lives of those He has called. "All The King's Men" is a clear and distinct call to every man to rise up, take their place, and embrace the full measure of authority and responsibility that comes with being a man of God.

As ambassadors for Christ, we are more than spectators in the world's affairs - we are active participants in advancing the Kingdom. We represent a King whose power, wisdom, and love far surpass anything this world can offer. It is our responsibility to show the world what Jesus is like - not through mere words, but through tangible, godly character reflected in our actions, decisions, and interactions. We are to be vessels of honor, carefully preserved and consecrated, carrying the light of Christ into every corner of our lives and society.

This book is written with the understanding that the life of a man is not meant to be passive or timid. God has created us with a divine purpose, equipping us with authority to take dominion over our circumstances. With His Spirit dwelling within, we are endowed with the courage of a lion, the discipline of a soldier, and the wisdom of a king. We are warriors in the army of the Lord, not just surviving the battles of life, but winning them by faith and divine strategy.

Prayer is our lifeline, and the words Jesus taught us to pray are not mere tradition - they are a blueprint for spiritual victory. Through prayer, we align our hearts with God's will, activate heavenly resources, and exercise kingdom authority over every obstacle and opposition. Our faith is not a timid hope; it is a powerful, unshakable force that triumphs over every battle we face. Every challenge, every trial, every setback becomes an opportunity to demonstrate the reality of God's power operating in and through us.

But faith alone is not enough. Determination and perseverance are essential. The race of life is not a short sprint; it is a marathon of obedience, endurance, and unwavering commitment to God's call. "All The King's Men" challenges you to run your race with intensity, to finish strong, and to fulfill the destiny that God has carefully prepared for you.

Throughout the pages of this book, you will discover practical instruction, biblical insight, and inspirational examples that will equip you to walk boldly in your calling. You will learn what it means to live with integrity, to exercise kingdom authority, and to impact the world for Christ in ways that are lasting and transformative. This is a book for every man who desires to rise above mediocrity, to embrace spiritual maturity, and to live as a man fully surrendered to the King.

The call is clear: God is raising up all men to stand in His strength, to shine as lights in a dark world, and to act as instruments of His glory. You are not here by accident; you are here for a purpose. As you read, prepare to be challenged, inspired, and equipped to step fully into your identity as one of "All The King's Men." The time is now. The Kingdom is waiting. And the King is calling you to rise up and take a stand.

# | 1 |

# "A TRUE MAN OF GOD"

Spiritually speaking, every real man of God is a mountain climber. Life is not meant to be lived on the comfortable plains of mediocrity or in the shadows of compromise. A true man of God sets his eyes on the summit, on the peak of authentic manhood, and he climbs with purpose, discipline, and unwavering faith. The path is steep. There are trials that test strength, winds that threaten to push him backward, and valleys that tempt him to turn aside. Yet, a man of God knows that every step, every struggle, and every sacrifice is a necessary part of the ascent. He does not climb for recognition, fame, or earthly reward, but to become the man God has called him to be - a man of integrity, courage, wisdom, and spiritual authority. The journey is demanding, but every man who chooses to climb in faith discovers that the heights of authentic manhood are worth every struggle. The call is clear: climb, endure, and ascend because God honors the man who dares to reach for the summit.

At the summit, he does not simply stand on a peak of personal achievement; he stands as a testimony of God's transformative power. He has conquered fear, mastered his weaknesses, and embraced the character of Christ. From that vantage point, he can see life with clarity, guide others on their climb, and fulfill his God-given destiny with boldness and compassion. He serves the King of kings and Lord of lords and knows that all the King's men are to walk in His footsteps each and every day of their lives. Jesus is the ultimate example of true masculinity. He came to earth as a man and showed us what to be like. He showed us how to be a friend, a leader, and a warrior. He was a servant leader "who went about doing good and healing all that were oppressed of the devil" (Acts 10:38). He was always doing wonderful things for people, helping them in their time of need. Keep your eyes constantly on Jesus for He is the man you want to be like.

Have the desire and ambition to act like Jesus and talk like Him as you go about your day. In the rush of life, it's easy to get distracted by the noise of the world, by ambition, comparison, or the pressures of daily life. But as a follower of Christ, you are called to a higher standard: to keep your eyes constantly on Jesus, the author and perfecter of our faith. He is not just a figure to admire from afar; He is the man we are meant to become. Let His words guide your speech. Let His compassion shape your actions. Let His patience and integrity influence your decisions. Desire Him and let every step, every word, and every choice you make be a reflection of His life within you. The world is watching, but more importantly, your own soul is growing into the image of Christ when you intentionally live this way. Keep your eyes on Jesus, not just as Savior, but as your ultimate example. The more you focus on Him, the more you will find that your life will begin to align with the One who made you in His image.

Submit your life to Jesus and ask Him to point you in the right direction your life should go. When you accept the Lord's invitation to follow Him, for sure you won't be led astray. As Jesus leads and you follow, you will indeed go in the right direction. Before long great things will be done in you and through you. This is what walking with Jesus is all about. Jesus is the example all real men follow for it brings clarity and perspective to every man who chooses to do so. For sure, He is worthy of imitation. Paul once referred to Timothy as "my true son in the faith" (1 Tim. 1:2) and the goal of every man should be to live in such a way that the Lord Jesus will say the same thing about them. Consider Prov. 25:13 (TPT), "A reliable, trustworthy messenger refreshes the heart of his master like a gentle snowfall at harvest time." May the Lord feel this way about you. The goal of your life is to be like a gentle snowfall - quiet, pure, and refreshing - arriving at just the right time.

Are you a true man of God? Are you one of the King's men? To find out, you must let the Bible be the mirror in which you view yourself. Let scripture show you who you really are. All men need a mirror to look at. Just like a real mirror shows you what you look like on the outside, you need to let God's Word be the mirror that shows you what you look like on the inside. A true man of God is not the same as the men of this sinful world. He is a man who has been set apart. He is a new creation in Christ, an entirely different person than he once was. 2 Cor. 5:17 (TPT) says, "Now, if anyone is enfolded into Christ, he has become an entirely new person. All that is related to the old order has vanished. Behold, everything is fresh and new." The Message Bible says, "Now we look inside and what we see is that anyone united with the Messiah gets a fresh start, is created new. The old life is gone; a new life flourishes! Look at it!"

A true man of God is a man who has been spiritually reborn, a new creation who has accepted Christ as his Lord and Savior. He is a child of God and God's Spirit dwells inside of him. He is a man who is on fire for the things of God. He is not cold, and neither is he lukewarm. He worships God with everything he has: mind, body, and spirit. He walks with God every hour of every day. He prays without ceasing and studies the Word of God daily. He has a relationship with God that is personal and very, very special. He has the same passion for God that David had. God said in Acts 13:22, "I have found David, the son of Jesse, a man after My own heart, who will do all My will." God's evaluation of David was not based on perfection, but on position. He had a heart turned toward God, willing to obey, quick to repent, and eager to please Him. Is that you? Are you a man who is forever doing God's will or are you wasting your life by continually doing your own thing in this temporary world that means nothing?

A true man of God is led by the Holy Spirit. He lives a holy life in the presence of a holy God. He lives to please God in everything he does every day of his life. Within him is a deep overwhelming desire to please God. He prays what David prayed in Ps. 51:10, "Create in me a clean heart, O God, and renew a steadfast spirit within me." Inside of him is an upright spirit that lives righteously and holy before God Almighty. He's in God and God is in him. Jesus said in John 15:4,5, "Abide in Me, and I in you. As the branch cannot bear fruit by itself, unless it abides in the vine, neither can you unless you abide in Me. I am the vine; you are the branches. He who abides in Me, and I in him, bears much fruit for apart from me you can do nothing." This is what it means to be a true man of God. He's a man who surrenders every aspect of his life to God. He wants to please his Lord and Savior with everything he is and everything he has and everything he will become.

Mark 12:30 says, "And you shall love the Lord your God with all your heart and with all your soul and with all your mind and with all your strength." A man of God does not live for this evil, temporary world and its passing pleasures. No, his eyes are fixed on the unseen world knowing what is seen is temporal and what is unseen is eternal. He follows the words of Prov. 3:5,6, "Trust in the Lord with all your heart and do not lean on your own understanding. In all your ways acknowledge Him and He will make straight your paths." All the King's men are not arrogant or boastful. They don't lie or break their promises. They don't show up to work late, and they never make excuses for their behavior. A real man doesn't praise God on Sunday and curse his neighbor on Monday. He doesn't boss his wife around but gently leads her and his family in true love like Christ leads the church. His Bible doesn't sit on the shelf gathering dust because he uses it each and every day.

A true man of God knows what the Lord requires of him and he does it faithfully. Micah 6:8 says, "He has shown you, O man, what is good; And what does the Lord require of you but to do justly, to love mercy, and to walk humbly with your God?" 1 Tim. 6:11 says, "But as for you, O man of God, flee these things and pursue righteousness, godliness, faith, love, patience, steadfastness, and gentleness." The Message Bible says, "But you, Timothy, man of God: Run for your life from all this. Pursue a righteous life - a life of wonder, faith, love, steadiness, courtesy." Vs. 12 (MSG), "Run hard and fast in the faith. Seize the eternal life, the life you were called to, the life you so frequently embraced in the presence of so many witnesses." A man of God who lives by faith is a warrior of Jesus Christ. He is always watchful as he stands firm in the faith. He is forever ready to go into battle at a moment's notice. A real man is a man who loves Jesus Christ with all his heart and might and follows Him daily.

All the King's men give themselves willingly in unbelievable ways for the advancement of God's kingdom on the earth. They're all in no matter the price they may have to pay. Live your life in such a way that the Lord will call upon you for the most difficult assignment even at the risk of being thrown into a fiery furnace or a den of lions. God told Joshua to be strong and very courageous and He's saying the same thing to you. Why? Because He wants you to be His "go to" man for the most demanding of tasks. The Word of God wasn't written just to inform but to activate, to motivate men to get up off their bed of slumber and go do something worthwhile with their lives. The world we live in, and especially the local church, need men of action, men of depth, and men of courage. They need solid men who have built their lives on a solid foundation. All the King's men live self-controlled, upright, and godly lives. They know there is a connection between doctrine and duty, principle and practice, faith and works.

A real man has self-control in all areas of his life. Biblical masculinity is when you control your emotions and live according to godly wisdom, godly values, and godly morals. God's Word says in Prov. 25:28, "Whoever has no rule over his own spirit - a man without self-control - is like a city broken into and left without walls." Prov. 16:32 (TPT) says, "Do you want to be a mighty warrior? It's better to be known as one who is patient and slow to anger. Do you want to conquer a city? Rule over your temper first." You must discipline yourself for the purpose of godliness (1 Tim. 4:7,8) and apply great effort to cultivate godly character and moral virtues (2 Peter 1:5). Discipline is a deliberate, daily choice, a holy training of the soul. Just as an athlete submits to rigorous preparation to win a prize, the man of God must submit to spiritual training to grow in Christlikeness. Paul reminds us that while physical training has some value, godliness holds value for both this life and the life to come.

Eternal rewards are shaped by present obedience. Discipline requires you to say no to lesser things so you can say yes to eternal things. It means governing your thoughts, controlling your appetites, stewarding your time, and ordering your life around the presence of God. Prayer, Scripture, worship, and obedience are not optional practices; they are the training ground where godliness is forged. Without discipline, good intentions remain unfulfilled desires. Godly character is not produced through passive belief but through active cooperation with God's grace. Faith is the foundation, but upon that foundation you must diligently build virtue, knowledge, self-control, perseverance, godliness, brotherly kindness, and love. Each quality strengthens the next, forming a mature and fruitful spiritual life. Spiritual growth demands effort. Grace does not eliminate discipline; it empowers it. The Holy Spirit works within us, but we must respond by cultivating habits that align with God's nature and character.

Godliness is not developed in moments of convenience but in seasons of perseverance. When you discipline yourself and apply great effort, you are declaring that Christ is worthy of your best devotion. Over time, these consistent choices will transform you into Christlikeness. What once required effort becomes your nature, and godly character becomes the visible fruit of an inward life surrendered to God. In the end, discipline and diligence are not burdens but are pathways to freedom. They shape us into vessels of honor, reflecting the character of Christ in a world desperate to see Him lived out through His people. Live your life with your eyes focused on Jesus. It is critical to remember that your pursuit of becoming a man is really the pursuit of a Man - the man Jesus Christ. Becoming one of the King's men takes time, thought, attention, and action. Commit yourself to continual and strenuous effort to be conformed into the image of Jesus Christ. Be a man committed to obedient action.

As the Spirit prompts you to respond, respond. The most important thing for you to do is always the next thing God tells you to do. More than ever, the world today needs strong, godly men in its midst, men who will carry heavy burdens, withstand great pressures, and move threatening obstacles. When called upon, a real man will use his masculinity to protect those who are threatened in his sphere of influence. He doesn't run when trouble comes knocking. Men of God have to be strong and courageous every day of their lives because the heavy weight of their masculinity is under attach like never before. The world today wants to feminize the very idea of manhood. All around the globe men are trying to be women and women are trying to be men. Masculinity is mocked. Femininity is diminished. Men are encouraged to abandon the very qualities God placed within them, while women are pushed to reject the grace and power of their own design. What must God be thinking?

All men need a mountain to climb, a dream to fulfill, a goal to achieve. Real men come to life by giving themselves a purpose to which they will spend their lives. A real man wants his life to count for something. He will only feel the full weight of his masculine strength when he aspires to have maximum impact in the world in which he lives. A purpose-filled man hates to be on the outside looking in. He wants to be in the game, not sitting on the bench. He knows if you aim at nothing, you'll hit it every time. The goal of every man should be to fight against mediocrity. They're to be aggressive in their manhood. They step forward and cross the lines their adversaries draw in front of them. They always take the offensive as they push back darkness and take new ground. They always reject passivity and are never afraid to go out on a limb and take a risk. Norman Mailer once said, "Masculinity is not something given to you, but something you gain. And you gain it by winning small battles with honor."

Manhood is not about appearances, it's about action. It's about the choices he makes that line up with the Word of God. In other words, a man is as a man does. John Wesley said, "Give me one hundred men who fear nothing but sin and desire nothing but God and they alone will shake the gates of hell and set up the kingdom of heaven upon the earth." Reaching the summit of authentic manhood isn't easy but it is a high and lofty goal. Abraham Lincoln once said, "Impossibilities vanish when a man and his God confront a mountain." Being called a man is a high compliment but just because you're a male means that you're a man. Like the Marine slogan, manhood belongs to the few and the proud. Real men are revealed and identified by their actions, not their anatomy. Saying you're a man means nothing if you don't have daily, godly actions to back it up. It is no secret that a good man is hard to find, a man who uses his influence to impact the family, his church, his community, and his nation.

All the king's men throw off sin and everything else that hinders their walk with God so they can run with endurance the race that is set before them (Heb. 12:1). Men of God persevere with patient endurance even when that can't understand or grasp onto the magnitude of all the wonderful things God has planned for them. They know God wants to do something great with their lives and when it does not happen right away, they refuse to let impatience overwhelm them. They leave everything in God's very capable hands and submit to His timing. They don't try to make things happen on their own knowing a moment of patience can save a lifetime of regret. Because the best things in life take time, all the King's men don't complicate God's plan with their own solutions but instead are prepared to wait on God for as long as it takes. The truth is, more times than not, it probably will take a long time. Abraham and Sarah waited 25 years to have a son and Joshua and Caleb waited 40 years to enter the Promised Land.

God is notoriously slow in our understanding of time. Remember, to Him a day is as a thousand years so when He says He'll so something soon, it could take a while for it to happen. The key to becoming one of the King's men is to never try to get ahead of God when He isn't moving fast enough for you. Don't create an Ishmael when God wants to give you an Isaac. Consider 2 Peter 3:9, "The Lord is not slow in keeping His promise, as some understand slowness. He is patient." The Passion Translation says, "His delay simply reveals His long patience toward you." Some men feel they're stuck in the middle of God's promise and it seems like their life is going in the opposite direction. Yes, patience can be painful at times so what do you do in the meantime? The secret to dealing with patience is found in Ps. 37:7 which says, "Be still in the presence of the Lord, and wait patiently for Him to act." You'll be able to wait patiently for the Lord if you'll learn to slow your life down, even if it's only for ten minutes each day.

Stop everything. Be still and know He is God. Understand that God is more interested in your character than He is your comfort. Go to a quiet place and listen to some soft praise music. Calm down and focus on how good God is. If you'll do that, you will calm the savage beast of impatience inside of you. As you meditate on Him alone, the presence of God will overwhelm you and slow you down. In your peaceful calm you'll become content where you're at in the race set before you. You'll know that God isn't finished with you yet and that great things are in store for your life. You'll soon reach the summit of authentic manhood and the devil better watch out. As you spend time alone with God, you'll suddenly be changed for the better on the inside. When you must wait, focus on what's happening in you, not what's happening to you. This is all about becoming one of the King's men. Yes, being patient has its benefits. Godly character is developed inside of you as you patiently learn how to wait on God.

# | 2 |

# "THE STARTING POINT"

The goal of all the King's men is to have a positive impact on this world. He forever strives to live a life of fulfillment, to leave a legacy by making a difference in the lives of others. The heart of every man carries a sacred longing to touch lives in a lasting way, to leave this world better than he found it. This desire is not accidental; it is planted there by God Himself. From the beginning, man was created with purpose, called to cultivate, protect, and influence the world around him. To live without impact is to live beneath that calling. A fulfilled life is not measured by applause, possessions, or position, but by obedience to purpose. True fulfillment flows from aligning one's life with God's design, from loving what He loves, valuing what He values, and serving where He sends. When a man walks in integrity, humility, and faith, his very presence becomes a testimony. His words carry weight. His actions create ripples that reach far beyond what he may ever see.

Legacy is not something a man leaves behind only at the end of his life; it is something he builds every day. It is formed in quiet decisions, unseen sacrifices, and consistent acts of love. A man leaves a legacy when he lifts the broken, mentors the young, stands for truth, and reflects the character of Christ in a world desperate for light. Influence is not about power over others, it is about responsibility toward them. The greatest impact a man can have is not found in how high he climbs, but in how deeply he serves. When he surrenders his ambition to God and allows the Spirit to shape his character, his life becomes a vessel of purpose. Through him, hope is restored, faith is strengthened, and lives are changed. The noble pursuit of manhood is to live intentionally, love sacrificially, and serve faithfully knowing that a life surrendered to God will always leave an eternal mark on the world. A life truly surrendered to God is never small, never hidden, and never wasted.

When a heart bows fully to Him, heaven begins to write eternity through ordinary moments. What seems unseen by the world becomes deeply significant in the hands of God, for surrender invites His power to flow through human weakness. A surrendered life no longer seeks personal recognition; it seeks divine purpose. Every word spoken in love, every act of obedience, every quiet sacrifice becomes a seed planted in eternal soil. Long after the moment has passed, the impact remains, lives are changed, faith is awakened, and hope is restored. God takes the yielded life and multiplies it beyond the limits of time. Such a life carries the fragrance of Christ. Even in suffering, surrender releases glory. Even in obscurity, obedience echoes in eternity. The surrendered soul becomes a living testimony that God still transforms hearts, heals brokenness, and reshapes the world one willing vessel at a time. History remembers the names of the powerful, but heaven records the lives of the surrendered.

When a life belongs fully to God, it leaves fingerprints on eternity, and the world is never the same. To be the type of man the world needs you to be, you need to first and foremost be a good man. Care about people and let them know you're concerned about their welfare. The absence of evil is not an automatic indicator of the presence of good. A man's goodness is not based on the bad things he doesn't do, it's based on the good things he does do. All the King's men are to be agents for good. Don't be nice to people once in a while and only when it's convenient for you to do so. No, be proactive in doing good all the time. This is how real fulfillment comes. It's when you live life beyond yourself, when somebody else's life is made better because they interacted with you that day. Real men wake up each morning and say, "Lord, what would You have me do today? Where can I make a difference?" Ask that and you'll be on your way to leaving a legacy.

Ps. 112:6 says, "A righteous man will be remembered forever." The Passion Translation says, "Their circumstances will never shake them, and others will never forget their example." To leave a legacy you must live your life with integrity. Prov. 22:1 says, "A good name is more desirable than great riches; to be esteemed is better than silver or gold." All the King's men build their lives on the foundation of integrity. It's when you live life at full capacity knowing that the stronger the man, the stronger his foundation. Webster's Dictionary says "integrity" is a 'firm adherence to a code of values; the state of being complete or undivided.' Integrity is a commitment to say it, do it, and live it. On the journey to authentic manhood, integrity is the starting point. It's the launching pad for any man who wants to be a strong, powerful, and useful man. All the King's men know that integrity is a quality of life that is developed over time by men who want to be the best they can be.

Jesus said in Matt. 7:24, "Therefore everyone who hears these words of Mine and acts on them, may be compared to a wise man who built his house on the rock." Notice the words "and acts on them." Building a firm foundation of integrity takes not only hearing the truth but also acting on it. You must do what you say you believe in. Be an honest man who always tells the truth. Be generous and share with others. Be courteous to people, walk in honor, and have a good work ethic at your job. Be a man of integrity and stand head and shoulders above everyone else. Instability and weakness characterize the man who lacks integrity. He's unstable in everything he does. Integrity enables a man to live among the people with the highest reputation. It allows you to function as the best version of yourself because you have nothing to hide. With integrity you can stand upright in full view of the world. Integrity must flow into every part of your life in order to maintain an upright status.

Integrity is the backbone of manhood. Without it a man can't function as the best version of himself. He can't function at full capacity. He can't be an upright man. Integrity allows you to live upright and in full view of others without fear, hesitation, or doubt. It's to live in full confidence that the world can experience the best version of you. Don't be casual when you bless other people but serve them with intensity. Don't be lackluster in the things you do but give it everything you've got. Be the best you can be. All the King's men are not spiritually lazy, complacent, and easygoing. No, they're intense and full of passion toward Christ, caring deeply about the work God would have them do. God Himself is intense. Deut. 4:24 says He is "a consuming fire." That's the type of fire that leaves nothing behind. It's intensity that pulls you out of your comfort zone. When Jesus came in the flesh, people were often surprised at the intensity of His teaching and His actions. He overturned tables and called the religious leaders unflattering names.

Rom. 12:11 (NIV) says, "Never be lacking in zeal but keep your spiritual fervor, serving the Lord." TPT, "Be enthusiastic to serve the Lord, keeping your passion toward Him boiling hot! Radiate with the glow of the Holy Spirit and let Him fill you with excitement as you serve Him." Always do your best with intense effort and motivation. Have the eagerness to do something good for someone else. Be forever ready to put forth maximum energy and effort. Eccl. 9:10 says, "Whatever your hand finds to do, do it with all your strength." Whatever is worth doing in your walk as a man is valuable enough to be done with enthusiasm and care. Be fervent in spirit. Be white hot in the things you do. The Greek word "zeo" pictures a man so enthusiastic about his tasks that he can hardly contain the excitement. His desire to accomplish God's work with excellence and enthusiasm is constantly boiling inside him, creating a Spirit-empowered diligence regarding his divine assignment.

All real men are in a daily fight against apathy, the lack of interest, enthusiasm, and concern for the things they do. It's apathy when they lose motivation to do the works of God. Yes, it's easier to slack off and coast a while but real men don't take shortcuts. They don't back off from their assignment. They're committed to do the work they've been called to do. The greatest battle men fight is against apathy. Pastor Stu Weber called this generation the "era of the soft male" referring to men who are weak and non-caring about other people. Men who are spiritually apathetic no longer get excited about the things of God. They find themselves feeling indifferent about what God wants to do in their lives. James 4:17 says, "To him who knows the right thing to do and fails to do it, to him it is sin." Notice the problem isn't ignorance since he knows what to do. No, the problem is apathy. He doesn't care if he does the right thing or not. He lost sight of the calling on his life and has fallen into spiritual fatigue.

The way to combat apathy is to reignite your passion for Jesus and do the very things apathy is trying to stop you from doing. Press into the Spirit. Serve the Lord. Read your Bible. Rom. 12:9-12 (MSG), "Love from the center of who you are; don't fake it. Run for dear life from evil; hold on for dear life to good. Be good friends who love deeply. Don't burn out; keep yourselves fueled and aflame. Be alert servants of the Master, cheerfully expectant. Don't quit in hard times; pray all the harder." The best way to fight apathy is to force it into submission. Confront it head-on and refuse to let it dictate the posture of your heart. Left unchecked, it dulls spiritual hunger, weakens discipline, and slowly shifts your focus inward. But when confronted, it has no authority of its own. You must push past your laziness and self-centered desires and refocus your attention on Jesus. Don't wait for motivation to appear but instead choose faithfulness and obedience even when your flesh resists.

Spiritual growth is rarely convenient. It requires intentional effort, prayer when you don't feel like praying, worship when your heart feels heavy, obedience when comfort calls louder. Every act of discipline is a declaration that Christ - not comfort - rules your life. Self-centered desires thrive when attention turns inward, but they lose their power when your eyes are lifted upward. Refocusing on Jesus realigns everything. When you fix your gaze on Him, on His sacrifice, His authority, and His love, apathy is exposed for what it is: a distraction meant to keep you passive and powerless. The more you behold Christ, the less room apathy has to remain. Jesus never called us to a passive faith. He calls us to deny ourselves, take up our cross, and follow Him daily. That calling demands action, resolve, and submission. When you choose to act in faith rather than wait on feelings, you break the chains of spiritual indifference. In that place of surrender and focus, passion is restored, purpose is revived, and the fire of devotion burns once again.

Real men always look for opportunities to be radically generous. This is what they live for. Jesus said, "What you do to the least of these My brethren, you do unto Me" (Matt. 25:40). Ps. 112:9 says, "They share freely and give generously to those in need. Their good deeds will be remembered forever.

They will have influence and honor." TPT, "Never stingy and always generous to those in need, they lived lives of influence and honor that will never be forgotten, for they were full of good deeds." Those who live their lives doing random acts of kindness will never be forgotten. This is what it means to leave a legacy which is the sum total of your actions that impact the people around you.. And when you do a good deed for someone, do so with humility. Don't pat yourself on the back. Don't call attention to yourself always playing to the crowd. Prov. 29:23 says, "Arrogance will bring your downfall, but if you are humble, you will be respected." You'll also be remembered and this is what leaving a legacy is all about.

Jesus said in Matt. 6:3,4, "But when you do a charitable deed, do not let your left hand know what your right hand is doing that your charitable deed may be in secret." When you help someone out, don't think how it looks to those who may be watching. Just do it quietly and in secret and God, in turn, will reward you openly (vs. 4). Prov. 15:33 says, "Humility and reverence for the Lord will make you both wise and honored." Before honor is humility. Know with certainty that God will never elevate a proud man. Christ's humiliation was before His exaltation and so it is with all the King's men. Charles Spurgeon said, "Let us be humble that we may not need to be humbled." Those who refuse humility often learn it through hardship. Forced humility comes through broken plans, exposed pride, and unmet expectations. God, in His mercy, will humble the proud not to destroy them but to restore them. How much better it is to choose humility willingly than to be corrected painfully.

The highest level of living is where your life impacts the life of someone else, when you go above and beyond the range of normal or merely physical human experiences. Many men live life by merely going through the motions which don't bring any fulfillment to their life. Their life has no meaning and they feel life would be better if they had not been born. What these men don't realize is that we are not the product of our circumstances or intentions, we are the product of our decisions. This is why right decisions must be made. There is probably no decision more important than when you decide to live your life on purpose, to live a life where you make a difference in your family, your church, your community. What should you be doing with your life? Consider what Jesus said in John 15:8, "This is My Father's glory, that you bear much fruit, showing yourselves to be My disciples." Vs. 11, "I have told you this so that My joy may be in you and that your joy may be complete."

Internal fulfillment will be on the inside of you when you help make the lives of other people better. You have to know what God wants you to do with your life. If you don't, your life will be in disarray. Prov. 29:18 says, "Where there is no vision, the people perish." TPT, "When there is no clear prophetic vision, people quickly wander astray. But when you follow the revelation of the Word, heaven's bliss fills your soul." Marriages fail and people commit suicide when they have no vision for their life. This is why you must know why God put you on this earth. A clear purpose for life will bring focus. You'll know what you're supposed to do and what you shouldn't do. It will also give you endurance when hard times come. Many men quit the race of life because their focus isn't clear enough. In other words, they don't know why they're here. Having a clear picture for your life is what brings fulfillment. Clarity of purpose, when you know where your life is headed, is what gives life its deepest satisfaction.

When you love serving God, you'll have a sense of fulfillment down inside of you. This being true, the question that needs to be answered is, "How do I find my purpose in life?" Consider Eph. 1:11 (TPT), "Before we were even born He gave us our destiny; that we would fulfill the plan of God who always accomplishes every purpose and plan in His heart." Before you were even born God chose you and predestined you to be one of the King's men. Neither fate or human merit determines your destiny. It is God alone who chooses your purpose in life. The Greek word "proorizo" means 'to mark out with a boundary beforehand.' All men are what they are because of what God chose to make them before any man was ever created. This Greek word was used in Acts 4:28, "But everything they did was determined beforehand according to Your will, according to the destiny you had marked out for them." God's purpose for your life was planned in advance way before the universe was even created.

God's plan is an intentional plan, a blueprint of how you are to live your life. Know with certainty that God has a plan for your life. The truth is, He has an eternal purpose for all things. He is a loving God and what He purposes will manifest His love. Ps. 16:6 (NIV) says, "The boundary lines have fallen for me in pleasant places; surely I have a delightful inheritance." TPT, "I'm overwhelmed by the privileges that come with following

You." Your calling is yours alone for God refuses to give it to anyone else. It's yours and if you don't do it, it won't get done. Don't leave this life having not done what you were called to do. When you have clarity for your life, Ps. 16:9 says, "Therefore my heart is glad and my tongue rejoices!" TPT, "My heart and soul explode with joy - full of glory!" One of the greatest revelations in your life is when you discover what your purpose is, the reason you are here. The TPT goes on to say, "Even my body will rest confident and secure."

When you know what your assignment is, no more will there be tossing and turning in bed at night. A tranquil calm will overwhelm you as you eagerly await the beginning of a new day. It will be impossible to not be joyful when you know the reason you were born. Ps. 16:11, "You make known to me the path of life; You will fill me with joy in Your presence." TPT, "Because of You, I know the path of life as I taste the fullness of joy in Your presence. At Your right side I experience divine pleasures forevermore." You're off and running now. Phil. 1:11 (CEV) says, "Jesus Christ will keep you busy doing good deeds that bring glory and praise to God." Not only do you know what your purpose is, you'll enjoy doing it. Eccl. 5:20 says, "God keeps him busy with the joy of his heart." NLT, "God keeps such people so busy enjoying life that they take no time to brood over the past." Be willing to let God use you according to His divine plan. Only do what is pleasing and acceptable to Him for that is the ultimate standard.

You are now at the trailhead of the journey you've been called to take. Now what? Eph. 5:14, "Be awake, you who are sleeping and come up from the dead and Christ will be your light." What do you do now? Wake up from your slumber and do something good for somebody. Do that and Christ will shine on you, opening windows of opportunity for you each and every day. Vs. 16,17 (TPT), "Take full advantage of every day as you spend your life for His purposes. And don't live foolishly for then you will have discernment to fully understand God's will." Every day is a gift from God - a sacred opportunity to live with purpose, to reflect His glory, and to make an eternal impact. Time is fleeting, and the moments we have are not meant to be wasted on trivial pursuits or self-centered ambitions. Instead, we are called to use each day intentionally, investing our energy, talents, and heart into what aligns with God's purposes. Let every sunrise remind you that today is another chance to serve, love, and honor the One who gave you life.

# | 3 |

# "VESSEL OF HONOR"

As one of the King's men, you are to be in faithful service to your Lord and Savior. You're not here just so God can meet your needs, you're here so God can use you to help meet the needs of others. You are not summoned into the Kingdom merely to be sustained by it, but to serve it. You are not enlisted so that heaven becomes a storehouse for your comfort alone; you are called so that your life becomes a vessel through which God's heart reaches a hurting world. The King meets your needs because He is good, but He also shapes your character because He has a plan and purpose for your life. Grace does not end with what God does for you; it begins again with what God desires to do through you. Every provision you receive is a preparation. Every blessing is an assignment. Every answer to prayer is an invitation to become the answer to someone else's prayer. True faith matures when you move from the posture of being a receiver to the posture of being a servant.

The King is not looking for consumers of grace, but carriers of it. You are strengthened so you can lift the weak, comforted so you can comfort others, forgiven so you can extend mercy, and loved so you can love without reservation. All the King's men understand that the kingdom of God advances through faithful service, not self-centered devotion. You must lay down your preferences in order to pick up His purpose. You are to deny yourself of what you want so that Christ may be revealed through you. Your life will then become a living testimony that the King is good, compassionate, and near. You are here on assignment. Chosen, equipped, and sent. Not to ask only, but to give. Not to be served, but to serve. And as you do that, you will discover a profound truth of the kingdom: when you pour yourself out for others, the King will pour Himself into you. This is the calling of all the King's men - to serve faithfully and to let the love of Christ flow through us until the world sees not us, but the King Himself.

2 Tim. 2:20 says, "But in a great house there are not only vessels of gold and silver, but also of wood and clay, some for honor and some for dishonor." The Phillips Bible says, "Some are used for the highest purposes and some for the lowest." TPT, "Some of them are used for banquets and special occasions, and some for everyday use." It is God's clear intention that every man be used in serving the Lord Jesus Christ. Sad to say, not all of them are the King's men and are not doing what God wants them to do. God has given gifts to every man to be used for His service but not everyone uses them on a regular basis if at all. They are not serving the Lord each and every day. Yes, having impressive abilities and skills are important and they do play a part in God's plan. They are not, however, the main feature when it comes to being used by God. Also,

having great knowledge of the Bible doesn't mean God is going to use you. You can be a Bible scholar and yet be detrimental to the cause of Jesus Christ.

So what type of person does God use? Who can rightfully be called one of the King's men? Paul reveals to Timothy that God only uses cleansed people who flee sin and pursue godliness. 2 Tim. 2:21, "Therefore, if anyone cleanses himself from the latter, he will be a vessel for honor, sanctified and useful for the Master, prepared for every good work." TPT, "Your life and ministry must not be disgraced, for you are a pure container of Christ and dedicated to the honorable purposes of your Master, prepared for every good work He gives you to do." The church is the great house Paul is referring to. This house is defined by the presence of God. It is the mansion in which God abides, the temple in which He is worshiped, the palace in which He rules, the place of defense for His truth. Where God dwells, that place becomes holy. Charles Spurgeon said, "It is a great house, worthy of the infinite heart of Jehovah, worthy of the blood of Jesus the incarnate God, and worthy of the ever-blessed Spirit."

The Church is holy not because of human perfection, but because of divine habitation. It is a great house because it is the house of the great God, the house where millions of people throughout countless generations have been filled with the great goodness of God. The church is a great house because of its importance. It is where bread and wine are given to refresh the weary and shelter to those who have been lost in the storm. It is the place where the sick and hurting are

nourished back to health. It is the place where the weak become strong, where their strength is renewed like the eagle's.
Within this great house are many vessels - some for honor
and some for common use. In God's mansion, purpose matters.
Position matters. Character matters. We are not merely occu-
pants; we are servants within the house, called to reflect the
order, purity, and glory of the One who lives there. The peace
of God comes when we realize we can be golden vessels in this
great house.

This mansion is expansive. There is room for the broken, the
growing, and the maturing. Yet every room is governed by the
same Lord. Christ is the cornerstone, the foundation, and the
head of the house. Without Him, the structure collapses. With
Him, the house stands firm, filled with glory. May we live as
vessels of honor within God's great mansion so that His presence is not only housed among us but revealed through us. All
men are called to be God's caretakers here on the earth, to fulfill His purposes and do His bidding. A servant is someone who
carries out the will of another. A golden vessel never fails to
accomplish the will of the Lord and the purposes of God. Indeed, they are profitable for the Master's use. Be encouraged
knowing God can use you whoever you are and whatever your
background may be. You can be a golden vessel of honor that
contains the glory of the living God.

A vessel of honor is not defined by outward appearance, position, or title, but by consecration. When you separate yourself unto God - choosing obedience over convenience, holiness
over compromise - you make room for His glory to abide. God

does not pour His glory into vessels cluttered with self; He fills those who are emptied of themselves and fully yielded to Him. You were designed to contain His presence, to carry His love, His power, His wisdom, and His compassion into a broken world. Just as the Ark of the Covenant carried the glory of God, you now bear His presence through the indwelling Holy Spirit. Wherever you go, the glory goes with you not for display, but for impact, not for personal elevation, but for divine purpose. Being a golden vessel means you are available to be used. It means your life becomes a conduit through which God heals, restores, encourages, and transforms others. The vessel does not take credit for what it carries -it simply remains clean, open, and ready.

Flee sin and pursue godliness and you can become the kind of container that God can use to present any and every kind of good gift to people for their blessing and God's glory. Allow the Master Potter to examine your heart. Let Him cleanse what needs to be cleansed and refine what needs refining. Yield yourself fully to Him, and say, "Lord, make me a vessel of honor." When you do that, you will discover the glorious truth that the same God who fills heaven and earth has chosen to place His glory within you. You are not common. You are chosen. You are refined. You are a golden vessel of honor, prepared to carry the glory of the living God. When God chooses to use you, He is not placing a crushing weight upon your shoulders - He is extending a sacred privilege into your hands. Being used by God is a great blessing and not a heavy burden. If you consider your service to others a weight you must carry you will lose heart and grow weary in well-doing. Never should you let this happen.

To be used by God is not a burden to endure but a blessing to embrace. Heaven does not recruit servants to exhaust them; it calls sons and daughters to partner with divine purpose. The moment service begins to feel heavy is often the moment your perspective has shifted. You begin to see people as problems instead of assignments, ministry as obligation instead of opportunity, and obedience as duty instead of devotion. When this happens, the heart grows tired long before the hands do. Weariness sets in not because the work is too great, but because joy has been replaced by obligation. Scripture reminds us, "Do not grow weary in doing good, for in due season we shall reap if we do not lose heart" (Gal. 6:9). Weariness is not caused by serving - it is caused by serving without love, without grace, and without remembering who it is you are serving. When service flows from intimacy with God, strength is renewed. But when it flows from self-effort alone, the soul becomes drained.

Jesus Himself said, "My yoke is easy, and My burden is light" (Matt. 11:30). That tells us something powerful. If the load feels unbearable, you may be carrying something He never asked you to carry. God never intended for you to bear the weight of outcomes, results, or people's responses. Your responsibility is obedience; the results belong to Him. When you understand that God is working through you and not merely using you, service becomes worship. Every act of kindness becomes seed. Every sacrifice becomes sacred. Every moment of faithfulness becomes an offering of praise. What once felt like a burden is transformed into joy because you realize God trusted you enough to be a vessel of His grace. So serve with gratitude, not grudgingly. Give with gladness, not heaviness. When God uses you, He is not draining you - He is blessing you. And those who serve from a heart of joy will not grow weary, for their strength is continually renewed by the One they serve.

Sad to say, there are found in God's great house some professing Christians whose practice is quite inconsistent with their profession. In other words, they're not who they say they are. Do not think it strange that in the church bad men are mixed in with the good. Matt. 13:25 says, "The enemy came and sowed tares among the wheat, and went his way." These tares are the vessels of dishonor, people who walk in darkness and don't cleanse themselves from sin. They talk the talk but don't walk the walk. Paul said in 2 Tim. 4:10, "Demas has deserted me because he loves the things of this life and has gone to Thessalonica." Demas was to Paul what Judas was to Jesus. Charles Spurgeon said, "It is not such a great wonder that there should be persons in the church who are not of the sterling metal of sincerity nor of the gold and silver of truth. Where beneath the skies shall we find absolute purity in any community? The very first family had a Cain in it and there was a wicked Ham in the select few inside the ark."

Jesus said in John 6:70, "I have chosen you twelve, and one of you is a devil." In the King's garden even the lilies of Christ grow among thorns (Song of Solomon 2:2). The Lord has prepared a vineyard, and made a winepress, and built a wall around it. He did all this and yet the little foxes come in and spoil the vines (Song of Solomon 2:15). In the church there are wolves in sheep's clothing (Matt. 7:15) and in the fisherman's net that is brought to shore there are both good fish and bad fish (Matt. 13:48). Until the time of judgment we will find tares with the wheat, dross with the gold, goats with the sheep, and dead flies with the ointment. Golden vessels are none of these. Let it be known that it is you, and you alone, who must choose the type of vessel you will be. Will you be a vessel of gold and silver for honor, or a vessel of wood and clay for dishonor? Always strive to be a vessel of honor for God isn't going to use dirty lives that are defiled with evil of any kind to serve the good news of Christ to the world.

Don't be a filthy vessel that God uses for dishonor. He raised up Pharaoh in Egypt and used him to demonstrate His power (Rom. 9:17) and He used Judas in His plan of putting Jesus on the cross. These two men were not puppets on a string who had no choice in the things that happened. Both of them were responsible for the terrible sins they committed. Paul makes it clear in vs. 21 that cleansing is your responsibility. To be a vessel of honor you must walk in the light, confessing all known sin to God. If you want to please the Lord who has made you His own and be used by Him in a very special way, you must separate yourself from all that is unclean. When you come home from a hard day at work, you use soap and water to clean yourself. They're the means of cleansing but you must make use of them by applying them to your body. Likewise, God provided the blood of Jesus as the means of cleansing us from all our sins (1 John 1:7). When we confess our sins, we apply the blood of Jesus to our dirty lives.

1 John 1:9 (TPT), "But if we freely admit our sins when His light uncovers them, He will be faithful to forgive us every time. God is just to forgive us our sins because of Christ." The man who cleanses himself from all iniquity comes out of the category of "wood and clay" and passes into that of "gold and silver." The bottom line is that all men have a choice in their usefulness in God's great house. They have the ability to make choices which determine what type of vessel they will be. In the King's banquet hall vessels of honor are the golden utensils that bring the best food and wine to the invited guests who are worthy of the best the king has to offer. On the other hand, vessels of dishonor are the dirty, cracked buckets that carry the leftovers to the garbage heap and are often discarded with their contents. David said in Ps. 101:6, "My eyes shall be upon the faithful of the land, that they may dwell with me; He who walks in a blameless way is the one who will minister to me."

God takes sin seriously and so should you. Paul said in 2 Cor. 7:1, "Let us cleanse ourselves from all filthiness of the flesh and spirit, perfecting holiness in the fear of God." Is. 52:11, "Run away! Run away! Get away from there! Do not touch anything unclean. Get away from it. Make yourselves pure, you who carry the vessels of the Lord." This is not a suggestion; it is a command that calls for urgent action. Take sin seriously and cleanse yourself from being a vessel of dishonor in God's great house. Charles Spurgeon said, "The Bible must be your chart, and you must exercise great watchfulness that your way be according to its direction. Let every man, whether young or old, who desires to be holy have a holy watchfulness in his heart, and keep his Holy Bible before his open eye. We can sin without thought but to obey the Lord and walk uprightly will need all our heart and soul and mind. Let the careless remember this."

In order to be a vessel of honor you must pursue God passionately at all times. 1 John 1:5 says, "God is light and there is absolutely no darkness in Him." In the presence of God, sin and darkness is a non-reality and has no authority over those who "walk in the light as He is in the light" (vs. 7). Pursuing God with all your heart and soul needs to be an active and earnest endeavor. Paul said, "I press on toward the goal for the prize of the upward call of God in Christ Jesus" (Phil. 3:14). Paul is saying it is the habit of his life to keep pressing on. It was a lifetime commitment that gripped his heart and guided all his words and actions. The Greek word for "press on" is "dioko" which speaks of 'an intensity of effort leading to a pursuit with earnestness and diligence in order to obtain.' It implies a continuing effort to overtake, reach, or attain a goal. Paul was a vessel of honor because he pressed on as he pursued God passionately, diligently, and relentlessly.

It means to run swiftly after, to hasten and press forward. It's a hunting term and gives us a picture of hound dogs on the hunt as they pursue the fox in a hostile manner. Do you want to get sin out of your life? Do you want to be a vessel of honor? Do you want the world to see the best version of you? Then pursue God passionately all the days of your life. Be zealous for the things of God. Have a burning desire to please Him in everything you say and do, a desire to fulfill His will and advance His glory in the world in every possible way. Have a zeal that presses onward and upward. Charles Spurgeon said, "The heart must be vehement in desire, panting continually for God's glory." Paul said he pressed on toward the goal. A goal refers to that which one fixes his gaze, whether it be a target at which an archer shoots his arrow or the finish line that a runner seeks to cross first. To press on means to bear down with every fiber of your being to obtain the goal you're pursuing.

The person who presses on sees nothing else but that to which he is hastening to obtain. Every day when you wake up remember there is a race to be run. Never forget that the goal of your life is not to please men but to please the Lord Jesus Christ. David Livingstone once returned from a mission trip and was asked where he wanted to go next. Without hesitation he replied, "I am ready to go anywhere provided it be forward." Amen to that. With an intense longing in his heart Paul labored perfectly to serve his Lord and Savior, to offer himself up as a burnt offering unto his God and to be used by Him. Every day he cultivated in his heart a deep passion to promote the glory of God with everything at his disposal. He longed to hear the words, "Well done, good and faithful servant." Paul pressed on to be a vessel of honor, and you should do the same. Strive with all that is in you to serve in the banquet hall of the great King of the universe.

God imparts service in His great house to those who press on and strive for the opportunity to do so. Be focused and single minded, desiring every action you take to be a blessing to someone else. J. C. Ryle said, "A zealous man is a man who only sees one thing, he cares for one thing, he is swallowed up in one thing, and that one thing is to please God." It is by excessive zeal that we have less of earth and so much more of heaven. John Wesley said, "Get on fire for God and men will come and see you burn." The 18th century revivalist preacher Jonathan Edwards vowed before the age of twenty "to do whatever I think to be most to the glory of God and for the good and advantage of mankind in general." He vowed "to never do any manner of thing, whether in soul or body less or more, but what tends to the glory of God, to live with all my might while I do live. We should make the perfection of heaven our mark, to be laboring continually nearer and nearer to it."

Paul pressed on because his desire to serve God with all he had was the controlling factor in his life. He was forever reaching out toward the spiritual goal of service and blessing. Bible commentator Matthew Henry said, "Those who have heaven in their eye must still be pressing forward to it in holy desires and hopes, and constant endeavors and preparations." Paul said that all the King's men are "sanctified and useful for the Master." This means you've been set apart to be used by God when you dedicate your service and loyalty to Him. The Greek word for "useful" is "euchrestos" and means 'to furnish what is needed; easy to make use of; serviceable.' It pertains to being helpful, beneficial, and very profitable. You know that an honorable vessel is to be kept pure if it is to continue to be used. A useful vessel of honor does not get involved in the sinful things of this world but instead makes choices to remain holy and stay away from things that would defile him. Do that and you will be "prepared for every good work."

Your heart is pure and you remain in a condition of readiness to be called into service for the King at a moment's notice. The cleansed vessel is waiting for the Master to pull it off the shelf and put it to honorable use. He is forever ready and doesn't need to be urged, coaxed, or persuaded. Martin Luther said, "Oh, it is a living, busy, active, mighty thing, this faith, and so it is impossible for it not to do good works incessantly. He who does not these works is a faithless man." You are a vessel of honor and your willingness and eagerness to be used in God's kingdom is known by the Lord above and He will definitely use you in a special and mighty way. Eph. 2:10 (NLT) says, "For we are God's masterpiece. He has created us anew in Christ Jesus so we can do the good things He planned for us long ago." Being prepared shows how useful you are to the Master and that you are fit for every type of service. A vessel of honor is always ready, willing, and able. Does this describe you?

# | 4 |

# "CHANGE THE WORLD"

The goal of all the King's men has never been comfort, applause, or self-preservation - it has always been transformation. Heaven does not send men into the earth to blend in with darkness, but to confront it with light. Every man who belongs to the King carries an assignment: to change the world he lives in by reflecting the nature, authority, and heart of God. God is not looking for passive believers or silent spectators. He is raising up men who understand that the kingdom of God is not just a belief system, but a governing reality. Real men in God's kingdom are empowered by His Spirit and equipped by His Word to bring order where there is chaos, hope where there is despair, and truth where deception has taken root. The King equips His men before He sends them. He forges character in secret places, builds courage through obedience, and sharpens discernment through intimacy with Him. Strength in the kingdom is not measured by dominance, but by submission to God's will.

All the King's men are called to make a positive difference - first in their own hearts, then in their homes, and ultimately in the world around them. When a man allows God to rule within him, he becomes a vessel through which heaven can touch earth. His words carry weight, his actions carry purpose, and his life becomes a living testimony of the power of God. This world does not need louder opinions; it needs transformed men. Men who will stand when others compromise. Men who will serve when others seek status. Men who will love sacrificially, lead courageously, and live righteously. These are the men God empowers. These are the men He entrusts with influence. When all the King's men rise to their calling, cities shift, families are restored, and generations are changed. The world is not waiting for perfect men - it is waiting for yielded men. And when a man fully yields to the King, he becomes an agent of divine change, sent to make the world look a little more like heaven.

We are in the world but not of the world (John 17:14). We are no longer ruled by sin nor are we bound by the principles of this heathen world. But we are here for a reason. Our purpose in life is to be a shining light to those who are in spiritual darkness. Jer. 15:19 (NLT) says, "You are to influence them; do not let them influence you." Paul said the same thing when he wrote to the Corinthian church. He said in 2 Cor. 10:13 (ESV), "The area of influence God assigned to us is to reach you." Phillips Bible, "We shall not make any wild claims but simply judge ourselves by that line of duty which God has marked out for us, and that work includes our work on your behalf." Paul then said in vs. 15,16 (ESV), "Our hope is that as your faith increases, our area of influence among you may be greatly enlarged so that we may preach the gospel in lands beyond you." All the King's men know that "to whom much is given, much will be required" (Luke 12:48).

This statement is not a warning meant to burden the believer, but a revelation meant to awaken the soul. It reminds us that God never gives without purpose, and He never blesses without expectation. Every gift from God - whether spiritual insight, material provision, influence, time, or opportunity - carries with it a sacred trust. We are not owners of what we possess; we are stewards. The measure of our blessing is directly tied to the measure of our accountability. This means God never blesses you or gives you influence for your own benefit. If you have been blessed with talents, wealth, knowledge, time, and the like, you are held responsible to use all these blessings you did not earn to benefit others. Indeed, those greatly blessed by God will be held to a higher standard. Charles Spurgeon said, "Be not content to have rendered some service, but look for proportionate service." In other words, beware of doing little when you've been given much.

To change the world you have to be a good steward of the influence God has given you. Do not take lightly the power you have to help make the lives of other people better. See yourself as a world changer. See yourself upsetting the status quo of this godless world system. Believe you have the power and influence to turn this world upside down (Acts 17:6). You don't become like the world in order to influence people. No, you stand out and be different. The men who change the world are the ones who do not let the world change them. You're not here to please the world, you're here to upset the world. You're here to throw people off balance, to cause them to lose the stability they have in sensual pleasures. When all the King's men go into action - when men stop living as spectators and begin living as ambassadors - a holy revolution is set in motion both in the life of the individual and in the life of society. The world turned upside down is now right side up.

Society is changed not merely by laws or movements, but by men who carry the nature of the King into every sphere of life. In homes, marriages are restored. In workplaces, excellence and honesty raise the standard. In communities, love replaces division, and hope displaces despair. Wherever the King's men walk in obedience, the atmosphere shifts, because the kingdom of God is near. John Phillips said, "Wherever Paul went, things happened. Souls were saved, people took sides, feelings were stirred, decisions were made, the lines were drawn." May all the men of God be just as effective today. May they be like Jesus who once called a man a fool because he had done nothing to get his life right with God (Luke 12:20). Changing the world is not the assignment of the weak, the timid, or the ill-prepared. It is the calling of those who have been forged in the secret place, strengthened by truth, and anchored in unshakable conviction.

God never sent the unprepared into battle and called it faith. He sends the trained, the disciplined, the obedient - those who have learned how to hear His voice, submit their will, and endure resistance without losing heart. Before David faced

Goliath publicly, he faced lions and bears privately. Before authority was displayed, character was formed. Before influence was granted, faithfulness was proven. Timidity cannot confront strongholds. Fear cannot confront deception. Passivity cannot confront darkness. The world is not changed by those who hope things improve, but by those who are willing to be transformed themselves first - renewed in mind, fortified in spirit, and grounded in truth. Preparation is not optional. Prayer sharpens discernment. The Word builds spiritual muscle. Obedience develops endurance. Trials refine courage. Every season of hidden growth is equipping you for visible impact. What feels like delay is often divine training.

God is not looking for spectators; He is raising standard-bearers. Not those who shrink back at resistance, but those who advance with humility and holy boldness. Timidity cannot confront strongholds. Fear cannot confront deception. Passivity cannot confront darkness. The world does not need softer convictions - it needs stronger men. If you are willing to be strengthened, disciplined, and refined, you are being prepared for influence. Because changing the world requires more than passion - it requires power, maturity, and unwavering faith. Let it be known that being different from everyone else may make you unpopular and provoke hostility in some people. At the same time, your different way of living will powerfully attract others. They'll be drawn to you and want what you have when you share the Word with boldness. All the King's men are to be like walking torches who aren't afraid to share their faith, to spread the good news, to praise their Lord, to set their world on fire.

Jesus said in Matt. 5:13, "You are the salt of the earth." Salt makes food taste better. Don't tell people to turn or burn. No, take your influence and bless people into the kingdom. Rom. 2:4 says it's "the goodness of God that leads you to repentance." TPT, "The wealth of His extravagant kindness is meant to melt your heart and lead you into repentance." Oh yes, God is a good God and, more times than not, the only way the world experiences and comes to know His goodness is through the words and actions of His holy people. You get people's attention when you ask them, "What can I do for you?" They're not asked this by the sinners of the world and may be caught off guard at first. But that's okay. They'll come around when they see the sincerity in your heart as you converse with them. Just be real. Let your light shine and watch what happens. Your light gives others permission to believe again and to hope again. People begin to see God, not because you preached a sermon, but because you lived one.

God loves the world, and it blesses Him when you love the world also. He likes it when you leave the ninety-nine sheep on the mountain and go in search for the one that went astray (Matt. 18:12). Your calling is to be the hands and feet of Jesus to the world He loves. Don't just tell people you love them, show them by your actions that your love and God's love is real and genuine. Make the Lord's business your business. Heb. 13:16 (GWT) says, "Don't forget to do good things for others and to share what you have with them. These are the kinds of sacrifices that please God." Charles Spurgeon said, "Let your gift be an outburst of a free and gracious spirit which takes delight in showing that it does not praise God in word only, but in deed and in truth." Just as God is forever doing good, so also should you do good to others, to give of your own good things to those who need them, and to do this at some sacrifice to yourself.

St. Francis of Assisi said, "Preach the Gospel and, if necessary, use words." Wherever you go, find a need and fill it, find a hurt and heal it. This is how you preach the gospel. It is now time to change the world. You have your own sphere of influence where you can make a difference. And when you change your world, you help change the world. Jesus said in Matt. 5:14 (TLB), "You are the world's light, a city on a hill, glowing in the night for all to see." Notice what He says next, "Don't hide your light!" TPT says, "Your lives light up the world." Vs. 16 (TLB), "Let it shine for all, let your good deeds glow for all to see, so that they will praise your heavenly Father." If you have breath in your lungs, God can and will use you to influence the people in your world. The same way God impacted your life, you'll be able to impact the life of others. All the King's men have their own sphere of influence; people they're in close contact with on a regular basis. This includes their family, friends, classmates, co-workers, and fellow church members.

Studies show that the number of people you spend at least an hour with each week is twelve. These are the people in your sphere of influence and they're not there by accident. What does Jesus say you should do with these people? Mark 5:19, "Go home to your family and friends. Tell them how much the Lord has done for you and how He has had mercy on you." Witness to them how God has changed your life. Don't beat them over the head telling them how they have to change. Just tell them the difference God made in your life. Be a witness wherever you may be. It is no accident you are where you are. Acts 17:26 says God "has determined their preappointed times and the boundaries of their habitation." Wherever you're at, you're there on purpose. Take advantage of the opportunity you've been given at whatever place you find yourself. Expect God to use you and He will use your life to illuminate paths, heal wounds, and draw people to Himself.

You're in the ministry and those in your sphere of influence is your congregation. You're their shepherd and they're the sheep you're to feed and protect. See yourself making a difference. Pray out loud the words of Ps. 90:17, "May the favor of the Lord rest upon us; establish the work of our hands for us." The Passion Translation says, "O Lord our God, let Your sweet beauty rest upon us. Come work with us and then our works will endure; You will give us success in all we do." Don't think you work at your job just so you can pay your bills. No, you're there to change lives. Look at it this way: Your vocation is your ministry location. Live your life in such a way that people will want to hear what you have to say. Be kind to people and always mind your manners. Display godly character at all times. Be gracious when you talk to people. Col. 4:6 says, "Let your conversation be always full of grace, seasoned with salt, so that you may know how to answer everyone."

1 Thess. 4:11,12 says, "Make it your ambition to lead a quiet life, to mind your own business and to work with your hands so that your daily life may win the respect of outsiders." This

is how you draw people in. Live and speak in a manner that will invite others to Christ. This will stir people to ask questions, and you'll be able to share the gospel with them. Never forget that you represent the King of kings and Lord of lords. When you bring the presence of Christ to your sphere of influence, for sure you can change the world. God will give you opportunities to speak to people about Him. On purpose He'll cause somebody's path to cross your path and you must recognize when that happens. These are divine appointments and they're not by accident. Some person needs to hear something you have to say and it will be a tragedy if you let that opportunity pass you by. Do not underestimate the power of a timely word spoken in faith. One sentence can redirect a destiny. One act of courage can break years of despair.

Speak when the Spirit prompts you to speak. Step forward when fear tells you to step back. The tragedy is not saying the wrong thing - the tragedy is saying nothing at all when love calls you to speak. You were not placed where you are by chance. Someone needs what God put in you. And now may be the moment they've been waiting for. If you withhold what God has entrusted to you, the loss is not only yours. A door remains unopened. A burden remains heavy. A life remains one conversation away from change. Heaven may have already scheduled the intersection, and your voice is the deciding factor. Be led by the Spirit and listen for His direction. Do that and you'll be at the right place at the right time. Prov. 16:9 says, "In his heart a man plans his way, but the Lord directs his steps." That phone call you got was not a mistake. It was an opportunity for you to change the world. Things like this happen more times than people realize.

Start changing the way you see things. Consider every encounter you have with people as your God-given chance to impact their life. And when these divine encounters do happen, have a message in your heart prepared for you to share with them. Know ahead of time what you're going to say. The Message Bible says in 1 Peter 3:15, "Be ready to speak up and tell everyone who asks why you're living the way you are, and always with the utmost courtesy." Always know what you believe and why you believe it. And you should always be ready, willing, and able, at a moment's notice, to explain what you believe to someone else. Have your answer ready in a few plain, simple sentences. In a gentle and modest spirit, share with them your confession of faith all to the praise and glory to God. Don't give these people an hour-long sermon but share your testimony in three minutes or less. The last thing you want is to lose their attention because you talked too much.

All believers have the ministry of reconciliation. 2 Cor. 5:18 (TPT) says, "And God has made all things new and reconciled us to Himself and gives us the ministry of reconciling others to God." When you got born again, you were reconciled to God and now, as one of the King's men, you are to be messengers of reconciliation to those you come in contact with. The AMP says God "brought us into harmony with Himself and gave to us the ministry of reconciliation that by word and deed we might aim to bring others into harmony with Him." The Message Bible says God is "giving the world a fresh start by offering forgiveness of sins. God has given us the task of telling every-one what He is doing." When Jesus first called His disciples He told them right away they would be used to impact other peo-ple's lives. He said, "Come, follow Me, and I will make you fish-ers of men" (Mark 1:17). He later said in Acts 1:8, "You will be My witnesses in Jerusalem, and in all Judea and Samaria and to the ends of the earth."

In other words, you will be witnesses wherever you go. Today, the world is changed when all the King's men go into their world, into their sphere of influence, and make an impact on it. And how is this done? One person at a time. People aren't changed with information; they're changed when you have a relationship with them. They won't care what you know un-til they know that you care. Relationships set you up for con-versations. People get comfortable being around you and are now willing to open up to you and share some of the bur-dens they're going through. In those settings where relation-ships are formed comes the opportunity for the truth of God's Word to come out and, as a result of that, lives get changed forevermore. Understand that it is your destiny to help change the world. You do that by not just reading your Bible but by living it, by letting your light shine in a dark and confused world. This isn't going to happen without some work on your part.

Don't be lazy but get up off your easy chair and put some effort into what you're supposed to be doing. 2 Tim. 4:5 (NLT) says, "Work at telling others the Good News, and fully carry out the ministry God has given you." TPT, "Carry in your heart the passion of your calling." God is going out of His way to put certain people around you so you can touch their lives. The problem is if you're not looking for them, you probably won't see them. Don't complicate things. Just be aware that this is your ministry. God is expecting you to change the world. Know that people's lives can be lost if you let Him down. Rom. 10:14,15 asks, "How can they hear the message of life if there is no one there to proclaim it? And how can the message be proclaimed if messengers have yet to be sent? How beautiful are the feet of those who bring good news!" TPT, "How welcome is the arrival of those proclaiming the joyful news of peace and of good things to come!" The question to be asked is, "How beautiful are your feet?"

Are you proclaiming the Good News? 2 Cor. 5:20 says, "We are Christ's ambassadors; God is making His appeal through us." God wants all people to get saved and set free from all their afflictions. He is tenderly pleading with them directly through the words that come out of your mouth. Your responsibility is to tell people how good God is. He's been good to you and He'll be good to them also. Plant the seed in their hearts and God will make it grow abundantly. A mighty work is being done around the world and God wants you to be a part of it. Submit to Him today and give Him permission to use you to help change this sinful world. Walk in love and the rest of the fruit of the Spirit (Gal. 6:22,23) and people will become receptive to what you say to them. They'll soon consider what their life is like now and what it could be. Any life without God in it always leads to misery and people know everything else they've tried to live a good life doesn't work. Now here you are with the answer they're looking for.

# | 5 |

# "THE FRUIT OF THE SPIRIT-PART 1"

If you want to be a vessel of honor and help change the world, it is imperative that you walk in the fruit of the Spirit, those nine virtues that are evidence of being led by the Spirit. God does not first shape what we do; He shapes who we are. A vessel of honor is one that has been yielded, cleansed, and continually filled with the life of the Spirit. All the King's men are not those who shine the brightest, but those who flow the purest. God is not looking for impressive containers; He is looking for surrendered ones. When the fruit of the Spirit is cultivated within us, we become trustworthy carriers of His presence. Our lives preach before our mouths ever open. The world does not need more religious noise - it needs men whose character reflects heaven, whose responses reveal Christ, and whose lives quietly but powerfully transform their surroundings. When we walk in the fruit of the Spirit, we become living proof that God is at work, and through such vessels, the world is changed one heart at a time.

Gal. 5:22,23 says, "The fruit of the Spirit is love, joy, peace, longsuffering, kindness, goodness, faithfulness, gentleness, self-control. Against such there is no law." All of these fruits are to be found in the life of a man of God. Charles Spurgeon said, "Oh, that every one of us might have a vineyard in his bosom and yield abundance of the fruit of the Spirit." Nine parts of one fruit, all supplied by the Holy Spirit, covers your complete responsibility toward God, your duty toward your fellow man, and your duty toward your own self. Love, joy, and peace join you to God. Patience, kindness, and goodness reaches out to others. Faithfulness, gentleness, and self-control describe your inner character. The fruit of the Spirit produce in you the noblest of Christian character. Godly character is Christ's excellency reproduced by the Spirit in a renewed life. These nine virtues illustrate the character of Jesus, and it is His life that the Spirit produces in all the King's men.

Why walking in the fruit of the Spirit is so important is these virtues will make you more like Jesus. In turn, the people in the world will want the God that is inside of you. The problem we face is that a lot of people are not rejecting God, they're rejecting our representation of God. They reason if God is like us, then they want nothing to do with Him. But when these people see the fruit of the Spirit manifested in your life, they'll see what Jesus is like and this will provoke them to embrace the doctrine and faith of Jesus. One of the purposes of the Christian life is to progressively allow the Holy Spirit to produce more and more of His fruit in our lives which in turn makes us more like Jesus. The fruit of the Spirit is the outward manifestation of Christ in the lives of believers. This fruit is produced by yielding to the sweet influence of the Spirit inside of you. How you live on the outside is evidence of what's taking place on the inside. We bear fruit so that others can be fed and helped, and that God can be glorified.

John MacArthur said, "Fruit is a beautiful bouquet of virtues." People are starving for these virtues. When they find them in our lives, they know we have something they lack. Martin Luther said the fruit of the Spirit "bring with them most excellent fruits and maximum usefulness, for they that have them give glory to God." The kingdom of God is not a place, it's what God does inside of you when He's the King of your heart. Walking in the fruit of the Spirit allows you to walk in the best God has to offer. It's not about striving to become something you're not; it is about yielding to who God has already made you to be in Christ. When you allow the Holy Spirit to shape your attitudes, responses, and desires, you begin to experience life the way God intended it to be lived - full, free, and fruitful. The fruit of the Spirit are not mere virtues you try to imitate; they are divine qualities produced within you as you walk in step with the Spirit of God. As these qualities grow, they align your heart with God's nature and His purposes.

To walk in the fruit of the Spirit is to walk in the fullness of God's design. Knowing how to walk in the fruit of the Spirit can't be learned from reading a book. It's something that bubbles up from inside of you and manifests itself through your words and actions. Jesus said in John 15:4, "Abide in Me and I in you. As the branch cannot bear fruit of itself, unless it abides in the vine, neither can you unless you abide in Me." He went on to say in vs. 5, "I am the vine, you are the branches. He who abides in Me, and I in him, bears much fruit; for without Me you can do nothing." You need to realize that fruit is the byproduct of who you are. When you fall in love with Jesus and strive to be like Him, this fruit will begin popping out of your inner man. You'll become a vessel of honor ready to carry His presence, His power, and His purposes. Walking in the Spirit leads you into God's will, God's peace, and God's abundance where your life not only glorifies Him, but overflow with blessing to others.

It should come as no surprise that the first fruit of the Spirit is love. We would expect that because God is love (1 John 4:8). It's listed first because love is the greatest of all virtues. 1 Cor. 13:13 (NLT) says, "Three things will last forever - faith, hope, and love - and the greatest of these is love." This is why 1 Cor. 14:1 (TLB) says, "Make love your greatest aim." The love produced by the Spirit is not natural or conditional; it is divine in origin. It loves when it is inconvenient, forgives when it is undeserved, and endures when it is costly. This kind of love reflects the heart of the Father and reveals Christ to the world. Jesus Himself declared that love would be the defining mark of His followers - not knowledge, gifting, or outward success, but love. When love leads, everything else falls into place. Love shapes your words, governs your responses, and directs your obedience. It draws you out of self-centered living and into God-centered living.

The Spirit begins His work in you with love because love is the truest evidence that God is at work within the heart. Charles

Spurgeon said, "Love is a very practical virtue, and yet it is so rich and rare that God alone is its author. Only a heavenly power can produce it." Love is the supreme virtue and Paul alluded to this in Gal. 5:14, "For the whole Law is fulfilled in one word, in the statement, 'You shall love your neighbor as yourself.'" Love is also the well spring of all the other virtues. Joy is love in jubilation, peace is love resting, longsuffering is love enduring, and kindness is love with a bowed head. Goodness is love in action, faithfulness is love being steadfast, gentleness is love in refinement, and self-control is love obeying. Love also gives energy to faith for "faith works through love" (Gal. 5:6). Love is what the world needs to see preeminently in your life. They need to see you loving God with all your heart and soul, loving your fellow brethren, and loving the world around you.

Love is to be the motivation for all that you do. It's the main characteristic of your personal relationship with God and is a reflection of all you say and do. Love is a fruit of the Spirit growing out of your heart. True love comes out of a person because it is in them. It causes believers to not live for themselves but for the good of others. It is through love that we feed the hungry, clothe the naked, nurse the sick, visit those in prison, and take care of the homeless, the fatherless, and the widows. It doesn't matter if people deserve to be loved or not. True love flows to the deserving and undeserving alike. It is the virtue of love that is given freely to others no matter what. Love is unconditional and sacrificial. True love, the kind that flows from God's heart, is not measured by what is deserved or earned. It is unconditional and given freely, without expectation, without limit. It's what reflects the very essence of God. It is the fruit of love that reaches the mourning heart and wipes away their tears.

1 John 4:7,8 says, "Beloved, let us love one another, for love is of God; and everyone who loves is born of God and knows God. He who does not love does not know God, for God is love." Love always seeks the benefit of the one who is loved. It's a love that means death to self and the defeat of sin since the essence of sin is self-will and self-gratification. Jesus said in John 15:12,13, "This is My commandment that you love one another as I have loved you. Greater love has no one than to lay down his life for his friends." Love is so important that God won't even let you worship Him if somebody has something against you. He said first be reconciled to them and then you're free to worship Him (Matt. 5:23,24). God is saying, "Don't talk to Me until you first talk to them." You can't separate your love for God and your love for people. You can't love God and hate people, and you can't love people unless you first love God.

Everybody matters to God and this is why you have to love people unconditionally. Gal. 5:6 (NIV) says, "The only thing that counts is faith expressing itself through love." Theologian Isaac Newton said love "fills the bosom with such an attitude and desire for the good of others that it propels its carrier into acts of selfless service for others without strings attached. It is an attitude which leads to action. Love puts others before itself for the sheer delight of manifesting devotion to Christ by serving others as Christ did." Love is an attitude of selflessness. It is the very nature and substance of love to deny self and give to others. For sure, love is the greatest gift you can give to someone. Loving others is supernatural because love is the very nature of God. We can only love as God loves us when we give Him free reign to live and move in our hearts. When you fully comprehend everything God has done for you, almost immediately you'll find yourself wanting to serve others and make sacrifices on their behalf.

In time doing things to bless people will be as natural as breathing. Without even thinking about it you'll be loving, caring, tender-hearted and affectionate to others. The fruit of love is forever giving because it is completely unselfish. It seeks the highest good for another person no matter what the cost may be. 1 John 3:16 says, "We know love by this, that He laid down His life for us, and we ought to lay down our lives for the brethren." That is the pinnacle of what love is all about. As one of the King's men, it is natural to love because God's nature is now your nature. Where there is sacrificial love of willful choice, feelings of friendship and intimacy will overwhelm you. Love is spontaneous and always active. Day in and day out it does random acts of kindness to others. Love is the badge of discipleship and the landmark of heaven. It is impossible to love others with the love of God in one's own strength. It's a fruit of the Spirit and can only be exhibited by the power of the indwelling Holy Spirit.

What is so extraordinary about love is that it is the one thing that allows the invisible God to be seen in our world. God is spirit, unseen, beyond the limits of human eyes, yet when love flows through a heart, it becomes a living reflection of

Him. Every act of kindness, patience, forgiveness, and compassion is a window through which the world can glimpse the heart of God. When you love unconditionally, you mirror His perfect love. When you forgive those who hurt you, you demonstrate His mercy. When you give without expecting anything in return, you show His generosity. Love is not merely a feeling - it is a divine action, a force that bridges heaven and earth. It transforms ordinary moments into sacred encounters. Through love, the unseen becomes tangible; the eternal becomes experienced; the divine becomes known. Love is the light that reveals God's presence. To love is to make God visible not through grand gestures, but through small, consistent acts that echo His heart.

Jesus said, "He who has seen Me has seen the Father" (John 14:9). May all the King's men say the same thing. Let your love be the window through which others see the invisible God, and in doing so, you participate in His eternal work on earth. We serve a God who wants not only to lavish His love on you but also to overflow your heart with love so that you would reach out and do the same for others. God is love and He is always present. This means His love is always working in you and through you and is always available and at your disposal when you want to bless others. Learn to appreciate the simplicity and beauty of love for it is the supreme Christian virtue. Out of love flows the wellspring of Christlikeness and all that God is. To walk in love, you must first understand the depth of God's love toward you. You need "to grasp how wide and long and high and deep is the love of Christ, to know this love that surpasses knowledge that you may be filled to the measure of all the fullness of God" (Eph. 3:18,19).

The Passion Translation says, "The resting place of His love will become the very source and root of your life. Knowing this love is the only way to be filled with the fullness of God." As you ponder the great love God has for you, you'll find yourself treating people better. You'll start doing for others what God has graciously done for you. The kindness you receive becomes the kindness you give. Acts of love, once driven by obligation or duty, now flow naturally from a heart transformed by God's own love. The forgiveness extended to you becomes the forgiveness you offer. This is why it's so crucial that you receive God's love. The capacity to love others comes from the fact that you've already been loved by God (1 John 4:19). Make the choice to love people. Love is not an uncontrollable feeling you have, it's a choice, a decision you make. Before you can love people you must first choose to do so. Col. 3:14 (NIV) says, "And over all these virtues put on love which binds them all together in perfect unity."

Yes, love is supreme and must flow through every other virtue. As you pause and reflect on the vast, unending love God has for you, something within begins to shift. You begin to see not just His love and goodness, but His patience, His mercy, and His generosity poured out in your life. And when your heart truly absorbs this truth, it cannot help but overflow. In essence, the closer you walk with God and the deeper you understand His love, the more you become an instrument of that love in the world. The love that saved you, lifts you, and sustains you now reaches others through your hands, your words, and your heart. Let your life be a reflection of the love God has lavished upon you so that others, through your actions, may catch a glimpse of His boundless grace. Let your life be a testament to the world of His goodness, so that in a world that often feels dark and broken, people can witness the light of God's love shining clearly through your actions.

The second fruit of the Spirit is joy. Like all the other fruit, joy is a product of the Holy Spirit. It's the manifestation of the Spirit in the life of the child of God. Jesus promised supernatural joy to all His followers. He said in John 15:11, "These things I have spoken to you, that My joy may be in you, and that your joy may be made full." Jesus is the wellspring of all joy - the source from which true, lasting happiness flows. This joy is not fleeting or dependent on circumstances; it is the deep-down sense of well-being that anchors the heart. When you know that all is well between you and the Lord, when your relationship with Him is alive and vibrant, your heart is filled with a peace and contentment that no trial can shake. It is a joy that rises from the assurance of His love, the security of His promises, and the constant presence of His Spirit. In Him, the soul is satisfied, and even in the midst of life's storms, the heart can sing with the quiet confidence that comes from knowing the Source of joy itself walks beside us every step of the way.

The Father did not send His Son to oppress us with heaviness and sorrow but to cheer up our souls in Him. Zech. 9:9 says, "Rejoice greatly! Behold, your King is coming to you." Ps. 35:9 says, "Be joyful in the Lord." Paul said, "Rejoice in the Lord always" (Phil. 4:4) and Jesus said, "Rejoice because your names are written in heaven" (Luke 10:20). John Eadie said, "Spiritual gladness is the opening up of a new world and the hope of final perfection and victory. This joy is the spring of energy and praise wells up out of the joyful heart." The Christian life is to be a life of joy. It is founded on faith in Jesus whose life on earth began as "good news of great joy for all people" (Luke 2:10). It is with joy that God will welcome believers into heaven. The Master said in Matt. 25:21, "Well done, good and faithful servant. Enter into the joy of your Lord." Joy is essential, a vital part of the believer's life. Rom. 4:17 says, "For the kingdom of God is not eating and drinking, but righteousness and peace and joy in the Holy Spirit."

Joy is God's gift to all believers and is meant to be a hallmark of the Christian life. In the midst of adversity, you can have joy when you are aware of God's grace and relish His favor. Being joyful is good in all ways. It is good for God because it gives Him honor when we are joyful. It's good for you because it makes you strong. Neh. 8:10 says, "For the joy of the Lord is your strength." It is good for the ungodly for when they see Christians joyful they will long to be believers also. It's good for our fellow brethren for it comforts them and cheers them up. Joy changes things. You can change the world with a joy that is deeply rooted in the fact that inside of you is the living God. And when you are in Him, His joy is made complete in you. There is no joy to compare with that which flows from a deep, rich, and sweet relationship with Jesus. Martin Luther said joy "is the voice of the bridegroom and of the bride." It is a holy joy, rooted in knowing Christ. walking with Him, trusting Him, and resting in His unfailing love.

Joy is the inevitable overflow of receiving Jesus as Lord and Savior. 1 Peter 1:8 says when you "believe in Him, you greatly rejoice with joy inexpressible and full of glory." The Passion Translation says, "Through believing in Him you are saturated with an ecstatic joy, indescribably sublime and immersed in glory. For you are reaping the harvest of your faith." This joy is not dependent on circumstances, success, or comfort. It does not fade when trials arise or when the world disappoints. When we commune with Jesus, our hearts are satisfied in ways nothing else can satisfy. His presence brings peace to troubled souls, strength to weary hearts, and hope that anchors us through every storm. This joy is quiet yet powerful, gentle yet unshakable - born from intimacy, obedience, and surrender. The closer we draw to Him, the deeper the joy becomes. For in Christ, we do not merely find happiness - we find life, purpose, and overflowing joy that no one can take away.

God's joy is full and complete in every way. Ps. 16:11 says, "You will show me the path of life; in Your presence is fullness of joy; at Your right hand there are pleasures forevermore." Nothing human or circumstantial can add to God's joy or take away from it. But it is not fulfilled in a believer's life except through reliance on and obedience to the Lord. Charles Spurgeon said, "The command to rejoice is as undoubted a precept of God as to love the Lord with all your heart. The vows of God are upon you, and they bind you to be joyful." Joy is having a constant delight in God. It is a deep and abiding inner rejoicing which is promised to those who abide in Christ. It rests in God's sovereign control of all things. Joy is the triumphant overflow of Christian gladness and is the byproduct of obedience. Theologian Richard Sibbes said, "Those that look to be happy must first look to be holy." Get sin out of your life and discover the wonder of being joyful.

C. S. Lewis called joy "an unsatisfied desire which is itself more desirable than any other satisfaction." Ps. 118:24 says, "This is the day the Lord has made; let us rejoice and be glad in it." Joy is more than an emotion - it is a spiritual glow that shines from the inside out. When the joy of the Lord fills your heart, it paints your face with a bright smile that no circumstance can erase. That smile becomes a silent testimony, declaring that your hope is anchored in something greater than this world. Joy also gives birth to a fun, life-giving personality. It lightens your spirit, softens your heart, and allows you to enjoy people and moments without fear or heaviness. Even in serious seasons, joy brings balance - reminding you that God is still good and His promises still stand. From a joyful heart flow encouraging words. Joy guards your tongue from bitterness and fills your speech with grace, kindness, and faith. You begin to speak life instead of discouragement, hope instead of despair, and strength instead of fear.

Even as flowers thrive when they bend to the light, so also will shining, radiant faces come to those who constantly turn toward Christ. Your joy is a reflection of what heaven will be like. This is why every day of your life there should be glorious, triumphant, and heavenly joy. The Greek word "agalliao" depicts jumping and shouting for joy that cannot be contained. Does this describe you? It should. Everywhere you go there should be a smile on your face that lights up every room and a bounce in every step you take. A third century martyr wrote before his death, "It's an incredibly bad world but I have discovered in the midst of it a quiet and holy people who have learned a great secret. They have found a joy that is a thousand times better than any pleasure of our sinful life. They are despised and persecuted but they care not. They are the masters of their souls. They have overcome the world. These people are the Christians and I am one of them." What a great testimony to end one's life.

# | 6 |

# "THE FRUIT OF THE SPIRIT-PART 2"

The third fruit of the Spirit is peace. No matter what is happening around you, no matter what calamity seems to be shaking your world, you can possess a divine peace within you. This peace is not born from favorable circumstances, nor does it depend on everything going right. It is a peace that flows from a deeper source - the unchanging presence of God within your soul. Storms may rage on the outside, but when God reigns on the inside, chaos loses its power. Divine peace anchors your heart when uncertainty tries to uproot you. It guards your mind when fear demands your attention. It whispers assurance when the world shouts despair. This peace reminds you that you are not abandoned, not forgotten, and not overcome no matter how intense the trial. You may not be able to control the winds, but you can trust the One who commands them. When you surrender your worries to God, His peace settles over you like a calm after the storm - steady, secure, and sustaining.

It's true, a pandemic of stress and anxiety is attacking our culture like never before. Violent crime, economic downfall, and relationship breakdowns have everyone crying out for help and relief. People want peace in their lives but falsely assume they will have it when all their problems go away. No, the absence of conflict is not what brings you peace in its fullness. Biblical peace is the tranquil state of a soul assured of its salvation through Christ and it is not found in the absence of trial and hardship; it is found in the presence of God. Let the world do what it will. Let circumstances rise and fall. Still, choose to rest in the truth that God is with you, God is for you, and God's peace is greater than anything you face. And when that peace rules your heart, nothing outside of you can steal what heaven has placed within you. Jesus said in John 14:27 (NIV), "Peace I leave with you; My peace I give you. I do not give as the world gives. Do not let your heart be troubled, and do not be afraid."

The Greek word for "peace" is "eirene" and it means 'to join or bind together that which has been separated.' It means 'wholeness, completeness, inner-rest.' It also means 'fulfillment; without deficiency or lack.' Isn't that what everyone is searching for? The problem is they're looking for it in all the wrong places. You may not have everything you want, but the peace of God will give you everything you need. Yes, you can have a peace that will keep you calm in the midst of your storm. Peace is an essential characteristic of the kingdom of God. Acts 10:36 says, "God sent His word to the children of Israel, preaching peace through Jesus Christ, the Lord of all." Announcing the birth of Jesus, the angels declared, "Glory to God in the highest, and on earth peace among men with whom He is pleased" (Luke 2:14). Rom. 15:33 says, "Now the God of peace be with you all. Amen." This is saying God is the source of true peace. All other forms of peace are not real and counterfeit at best.

Not only is He the God of Peace, He is also the Prince of Peace. Is. 9:6 says, "And He will be called Wonderful, Counselor, Mighty God, Everlasting Father, Prince of Peace." He is also the Lord of Peace. 2 Thess. 3:16 (NIV) says, "Now may the Lord of peace Himself give you peace at all times and in every way. The Lord be with you all." Where is peace found? Under the lordship of Jesus Christ. You find it under the authority of His name and under the authority of His Word. Phil. 4:6, "Do not be anxious about anything, but in every situation, by prayer and petition, with thanksgiving, let your requests be known to God." Paul is saying to not be troubled by the hardship that comes your way. You can have peace in the midst of your storm and it all begins with prayer. Faith-filled prayer is your pathway to peace. The first thing you do when anxiety tries to creep into your life is pray to the Lord above. When you're finished petitioning Him for the things you need, thank Him for what He is about to do.

Sad to say, this is the part most people leave out of their prayers. They're quick to ask God for something but are negligent to thank Him for what they've asked for, for the blessings He has already promised. Many prayers are filled with requests but emptied of gratitude. People say, "Lord, I'll thank you when I see it," not realizing that faith gives thanks before the manifestation. Gratitude is not the reward for the blessing;

gratitude is the evidence that you believe the blessing is on the way. When you delay giving thanks, you reveal hesitation, doubt, and misplaced trust in what you can see. Don't wait for the miracle to praise Him. Praise Him because He is trustworthy. Thank Him because He is good. And honor Him because His word never returns void. Waiting to see the manifestation first is wrong. Thank Him now "and the peace of God, which surpasses all understanding, will guard your hearts and your minds in Christ Jesus" (Phil. 4:7).

The word "surpasses" means 'higher in rank.' The peace of God outranks your stress, your anxiety, and all your worries, concerns, and fears. The peace men have needed since the Garden of Eden is peace with God. Ps. 85:10 says, "Mercy and truth have met together; Righteousness and peace have kissed each other." The peace of God is the fruit of the presence of the God of peace in your life. When you have that, nothing that is happening to you will be able to take your peace away. Peace is tranquility in the soul, and you can only get it from God. Phil. 1:2 says, "Grace to you and peace from God our Father and the Lord Jesus Christ." In Eph. 6:15 the gospel is called "the gospel of peace." It makes peace with God, and it brings the peace of God. You are His child, and His peace is flooding your soul. Peace is the calm confidence that eliminates all fear, doubt, worry, and anxiety. Jesus said in John 14:1, "Let not you heart be troubled." He's saying don't worry or surrender to your fears.

Peace implies health, well-being, and prosperity. It is freedom from disturbance within the soul. It brings an inner tranquility of soul and spirit in the midst of adversity. The peace that God gives is not the absence of trouble, nor is it the removal of hardship from your path. True divine peace is the unshakable confidence that He is walking beside you through the fiery furnace of trouble. God never promised a life without storms, but He did promise His presence in the midst of them. His peace anchors your soul when circumstances rage, reminding you that no fire can consume what He is sustaining. When fear whispers that you are alone, His peace declares that you are never abandoned. This peace does not deny the reality of pain - it transcends it. It allows you to stand firm while the flames rise, knowing that the same God who walked with the three Hebrew boys still walks with His people today. The fire may test you, but it will not destroy you, because God is in it with you.

When you rest in this truth, anxiety loses its grip, and faith takes its place. You may feel the heat, but you will not be overcome, for His presence is your protection and His peace is your assurance. German theologian Hermann Cremer defined peace as "a state of untroubled, undisturbed well-being." Peace contrasts with strife and thus denotes the absence or end of strife. Real peace is reflected in the phrase "having it all together." When things are disjointed, there is lack of harmony and well-being. When they're joined together, there is both. Like love and joy, peace is unrelated to circumstances. A peaceful heart is not born from perfect circumstances, but from perfect trust. It rests in the unshakable promises of God, knowing that what He has spoken, He will surely bring to pass. Even when the path is unclear, the heart anchored in His Word does not tremble, because God's promises never fail. When you trust His promises and surrender to His purpose, peace settles deeply within your inner man.

In Mark 4, Jesus was sound asleep in perfect tranquility in the midst of a storm that threatened to drown everybody. Why? He had confidence they would reach the other side. He knew that the Father had a plan and would fulfill that plan. Confidence in God eliminates fear and gives you a peace that surpasses all understanding. When your trust rests fully in Him, fear loses its voice, because you know your life is not governed by chance but by divine purpose. Confidence in God does not deny the presence of trouble; it declares that trouble does not have the final word. Fear thrives where uncertainty reigns, but faith stands firm on the unchanging character of God. When you are confident in who He is, in His power, His love, and His faithfulness, you no longer feel the need to control outcomes. You rest in the assurance that the One who holds the universe also holds you. Confidence in God doesn't just remove fear - it replaces it with unshakable peace.

Your confidence in God releases a peace the world cannot manufacture or explain. It is the peace that guards your heart when circumstances are unstable, that steadies your mind when answers are delayed, and that anchors your soul when storms rage. It is the peace promised in Scripture - the peace that surpasses all understanding. When fear whispers, confidence in God speaks louder, saying, "He is with me. He is for me. He is forever faithful." And in that assurance, anxiety fades, hearts are calmed, and the soul finds rest not because everything is easy, but because everything is entrusted to Him. There is no human or psychological explanation for the peace of God. It just takes over and guards your heart and mind in Christ Jesus. That's the nature of the peace of God. Col. 3:15 says, "And let the peace of God rule in your hearts." The word "rule" means 'to exercise supreme command; to possess undisputed supremacy over.' It means that peace has a governing role in the life of every man.

The word "rule" takes on the role of an umpire, one who makes the final decision. In every moment of uncertainty, fear, or inner conflict, the peace of God is meant to have the final say. Pastor Kent Hughes observed, "How much misery we would avoid if we permitted the peace of Christ to umpire in our hearts, if it was the arbitrator of our lives." Theologian Adam Clarke said, "No heart is right with God when the peace of God does not rule. When a man loses his peace, he has given way to evil and grieves the Holy Spirit." Let the calmness of Christ rule over you when worry, fear, doubt, and other such passions arise. When peace rules in your heart, all is safe and all is well. Consider how Jesus was in control and moved into every situation with total poise. He remained cool, calm, and collected when other people were panicking around Him. Peace floods the soul when Christ rules the heart. Webster's defines "peace" as 'a state of tranquility or quiet, freedom from oppressive thoughts or emotions.'

The phrase "all is well" is translated from the Greek word for "peace." Commentator Kenneth Wuest says this peace is "that state of untroubled, undisturbed tranquility and well-being produced in the heart of the yielded saint. We have this peace to the extent that we are yielded to the Spirit and are intelligently conscious of and dependent upon His ministry for us." Charles Spurgeon said, "I have seen the Christian man in the depths of poverty not knowing where his next meal would come from with his mind unruffled, calm, and quiet. If he had been quite sure that ravens would bring him bread and meat in the morning, and again in the evening, he would not have been one with more calm. There is his neighbor on the other side of the street not half so poor, but wearied from morning till night, bringing himself to the grave with anxiety." He that has peace with God is covered from head to toe with the peace and serenity of God. No arrow of the enemy can pierce through this peace as you say, "All is well."

The fourth fruit of the Spirit is longsuffering. The Greek word "makrothumia" is often translated "patience" and literally means 'long temper.' Patience is a quiet strength that reflects the heart of God within us. A patient person is slow to anger, not because they are weak, but because they are anchored in trust and faith. Longsuffering is the ability to suffer long, to hold your temper for a long time. A patient person is able to endure much pain and suffering without complaining because they know God's timing is perfect and His purposes are greater than their understanding. In moments of difficulty, patience allows us to respond with grace instead of frustration, to persevere instead of giving up, and to shine as a light of hope to others. As James 1:19 reminds us, "Everyone should be quick to listen, slow to speak, and slow to become angry." True patience is not passive - it is the strength to wait, the courage to endure, and the wisdom to trust God even when the journey is hard.

The two root words that make up the word "longsuffering" is "makro" means 'distant; far away' and "thumia" means 'anger.' Combined together the Greek word speaks of a person who pushes his anger far away. The fruit of longsuffering is having patience with people who would otherwise make you angry. It is restraint that does not retaliate when others do you wrong. Yes, it is a good thing to have righteous anger for this is a sign of holy character. But it is wrong to get angry quickly at the wrong things and for the wrong reasons. It is important to know when to get angry and when to hold your peace, to know when to restrain yourself from becoming upset or speaking sharply to others. According to the Bible, anger itself is not considered a sin, but how you act on that anger is what matters. Eph. 4:26 says, "Be angry, and do not sin." The Passion Translation says, "Don't let the passion of your emotions lead you to sin. Don't let anger control you or be fuel for revenge, not for even a day."

This means that righteous anger against injustice is acceptable while uncontrolled or destructive anger due to a lack of patience is considered sinful. When you're walking in the Spirit, you're not vengeful or hostile. You don't have an emotional outburst because somebody offended you. No, your anger is far, far away. The lives of all the King's men are characterized by being slow to get angry. Their lives are marked by grace and lovingkindness with an eagerness to forgive. Longsuffering that is a fruit of the Spirit is not patience in a trial, it's about having patience with those people who have offended you in some shape or form. Longsuffering is the quiet strength of patience that endures without complaint. It is the ability to bear trials, offenses, and hardship without retaliating. It is not judgmental, is not abusive, and seeks not harm and vengeance. Bible commentator W. E. Vine said, "If forbearance denotes delay in executing judgment, longsuffering denotes the particular disposition which delays it."

This divine patience reflects the heart of God. To be long-suffering is to carry a spirit of mercy, to respond with gentleness rather than bitterness, and to trust that God's justice and timing are perfect. When you cultivate longsuffering, you become a vessel of peace. You resist the urge to fight back and instead allow God's Spirit to guide your response. In this endurance lies true spiritual strength: the power to remain loving, faithful, and humble, even when circumstances and people test you. Remember, longsuffering is not weakness - it is a deliberate choice to follow Christ's example, reflecting His patience and mercy in a world that often rushes to anger. Patience comes from a position of power. It brings self-restraint and careful thinking. As the Spirit produces patience in us, He is making us more like Christ. 2 Thess. 3:5 (ASV) speaks of the "patience of Christ" and Peter highlights the "patience of God" (1 Peter 3:20). We should all be patient even as He is patient.

Patience is the virtue that brings about forgiveness. You are to be patient and forgiving like God is. You are to endure offenses with a heart of forgiveness, compassion, and mercy. Num. 14:18 says, "The Lord is longsuffering and abundant in mercy, forgiving iniquity and transgressions." This is the patience of God. He is slow to get angry and full of grace. Longsuffering is the one virtue in the list most closely related to forgiveness. You are called to forgive, even up to seventy times seven each and every day (Matt. 18:22). John MacArthur said, "Never are you more like God than when you forgive. Never are you more like Satan than when you're angry and when you hate." Your life should be patience personified. You are not manifesting the fruit of the Spirit if you don't have patience with those who offend you and create havoc and chaos in your life. Where does patience come from? God is the source of patience, Christ is the example of patience, and the Holy Spirit is the dispenser of patience.

Walk in the fruit of the Spirit and you'll find yourself in a state of emotional calm and quietness in the face of provocation, misfortune, or unfavorable circumstances. Patience is the ability to hold your feelings in restraint and bear up under the oversights and wrongs afflicted by others. It does not hastily retaliate a wrong. With patience you'll have wells of endurance that will never dry up. You'll be able to keep calm and sustain continual effectiveness even in the face of unrelenting pressure. This is not so much a trait as it is a way of life. Charles Spurgeon said, "You will be hourly tried but the Spirit of God will give you patience to suffer long and endure much." Patience helps you endure the rudeness of others with a forbearing dignity and without complaint. It deals with unpleasant people with graciousness and fools without irritation. William Barclay says patience is "the ability to bear with people even when they are wrong, even when they are cruel and insulting. It is a great word."

Patience makes a man like God who is righteous, strong, and long tempered. Allow the Holy Spirit to manifest in you the fruit of longsuffering to be shown to others on the same level that God has been patient with us. Preacher H. Leo Boles said, "Patience is the even temper that comes from a big heart. It is loving tolerance in spite of people's weakness and failure. Love is patient and so must Christians be. The same divine quality that allows God to be patient with sinners enables the Christian to endure the exasperating behavior of others." You are to be patient in the sense that you show tolerance to others in love. Col. 3:12 says we are to "put on compassion, kindness, humility, gentleness, and patience." Regarding patience, vs. 13 says we are to be "bearing with one another and forgiving one another. Even as Christ forgave you, so you also must do." Who are you to be patient with? 1 Thess. 5:14 says, "Be patient with everyone." Nothing else needs to be said. Be patient all the time and under all circumstances.

## | 7 |

# "THE FRUIT OF THE SPIRIT-PART 3"

The fifth fruit of the Spirit is kindness. The Greek word "chrestotes" describes the quality of being helpful and beneficial. It is a noble virtue that seeks always to do good. All the king's men need to have the fruit of the Spirit on display in their lives for all the world to see, and there is probably no better way to do that than to be kind to people. Kindness is a noble virtue, born in the heart of love and expressed through intentional goodness. It is strength guided by compassion. Kindness chooses to see value where others see inconvenience, to offer grace where offense might be justified, and to extend mercy when judgment would be easier. At its core, kindness seeks always to do good. It listens before it speaks. It lifts rather than crushes. It heals wounds that words cannot reach and softens hearts hardened by disappointment or pain. Kindness moves beyond self-interest and asks, "How can I serve? How can I be a blessing to someone? How can I reflect the goodness of God?"

Kindness does not require recognition, applause, or reward. Its motivation is pure and seeks to bring light into dark places and hope into weary souls. A gentle word, a patient response, a helping hand, or a forgiving spirit can become sacred acts when offered in kindness. These simple expressions carry eternal weight, often changing lives in ways we may never fully see. In a world that often celebrates power, speed, and self-promotion, kindness stands quietly yet boldly as a higher way. It mirrors the heart of God, who is rich in mercy and abounding in love. When kindness governs your thoughts, words, and actions, you become an instrument of peace and a channel of divine goodness. To walk in kindness is to walk in nobility of spirit. It is a daily choice to do good, to love deeply, and to leave every place and every person better than we found them. God's plan is that the fruit of the Spirit be at work inside of you in such a way that it proves to the world that our God is real, that He is a loving and kind God.

Consider also that fruit reveals how healthy the tree is. In other words, it reveals how healthy your Christianity is and, more specifically, how well your walk as a man is. The lives of all men are to be marked by kindness. If kindness isn't sustained in your life, you're not a real man. Rom. 11:22 says, "Continue in His kindness. Otherwise, you also will be cut off." Your actions and choices do matter. Jesus said in Matt. 7:16,17, "You shall know them by their fruits. Even so, every good tree bears good fruit, but a bad tree bears bad fruit." Choose daily to be kind to people. Remember, you can't learn to walk in the fruit of the Spirit. It is the byproduct of who you are, the man God created you to be. Automatically kindness should be flowing out of you into the lives of other people. Prov. 11:17 (NIV) says, "Those who are kind benefit others, but the cruel bring ruin on themselves." Kindness is never wasted. It is not merely an outward act; it is a reflection of the condition of the heart.

Kindness aligns us with the nature of God. Scripture tells us that God is rich in mercy and abounding in love, and when we choose kindness, we participate in His character. Each gentle word, patient response, and compassionate action becomes a seed planted into the lives of others. In God's economy, those seeds always produce a harvest, often in ways we never expect. 2 Tim. 2:24 says, "And a servant of the Lord must not be quarrelsome, but be kind to all, patient when wronged, with gentleness correcting those who are in opposition." There should always be manifested kindness in the lives of all the true men of God. As a follower of Christ, you should be known for all the random acts of kindness you do. Archbishop Richard Trench said in the 19th century that the grace of kindness is "pervading and penetrating their whole nature, mellowing all which would be harsh and severe." He said that kindness "produces a goodness which has no edge, no sharpness to it."

Indeed, the fruit of kindness is indicative of a man who is Spirit-filled and fruit-bearing. Kindness is true, unadulterated politeness that reflects the love of God. It is the starting point as we work out our own salvation with fear and trembling (Phil. 2:12). Kindness provides for the helpless what they can't provide for themselves. It displays genuine goodness and generosity for it is the spontaneous overflow of love in the heart. Always be tenderhearted and impulsive in your kindness to others. Cultivate the artistry of showing godly love to those you come in contact with throughout the day. Kindness is love in action. It takes delight in contributing to the happiness of others by cheerfully gratifying their desires and supplying their needs. 1 Cor. 13:4 says, "Love is patient and kind." Charles Spurgeon said kindness is "consideration for others, readiness to help them in any way that we can." Kindness includes the attributes of loving affection, sympathy, friendliness, patience, pleasantness, gentleness, and goodness.

Medical science has proven that when you show kindness to others endorphins are released into your brain that makes you feel happy and gives you the sense of pleasure. In other words, you are hard-wired for generosity. These endorphins make you enjoy being good to people so much that you'll go out of your way to find someone to be kind to. Praise God for it is He who put those endorphins there. It is He who gives you the pleasure and the desire to reach out and help others live a better life. Wake up every morning determined to do kind things and say kind things to those around you. When you have the willingness to serve others, for sure the opportunities will be there. Be the type of person who is considerate and lets others go ahead of them in a line, one who is always ready to give a compliment, one who helps little old ladies carry their groceries out to their car. Have a way of thinking that leads you to do thoughtful deeds for others.

Be willing to give of yourself in love and mercy to others who may not be able to give anything back. Prov. 19:22 says, "What is desired in a man is kindness." Why does God want us to demonstrate kindness? Because He is kind (Ps. 25:6) and He wants us to become like Him. Biblical history shows that God's mercy and loving kindness was shown through the people He inspired. He always raised up deliverers and sent prophets to help the people. All the King's men are to be tools that extend God's love, mercy, and kindness to the world. They are to be a light on a hill that reflects the light of God's overwhelming compassion. Paul said in Eph. 4:32 (AMP), "And become useful and helpful and kind to one another, tenderhearted, compassionate, understanding, loving-hearted, forgiving one another readily and freely." The word "become" means 'to bring into existence.' This verse is saying you are to bring kindness to other people into existence. In other words, keep on becoming kind.

Paul is not calling us to arrive at a certain point in this life and in our behavior but to be in a lifelong process, a journey toward greater and greater Christlike behavior. You can help provide what other people need because you have the indwelling Holy Spirit to give you the energizing power to do what needs to be done. There is just a friendly nature about you. You're kind, caring, and make people feel comfortable. You treat strangers with warmth and respect as if you've known them all your life. Men who are friendly have a positive demeanor about them. They're always saying nice things about people and they bring hope and encouragement in the midst of troubled times. A friendly person is sociable and is easy to talk to and makes others feel valued in their presence. They approach others and include those who seem to be left out. The fruit of kindness causes a person to have tender feelings for someone else. They're easily moved to love, pity, or sorrow, to whatever is needed at the time.

The heart of a man who is walking in the fruit of kindness is always reaching out to others. They are so full of affection that their compassion for people moves them to the deepest depths of their being. The word "kind" comes from such words as "kin" and "kindred." To deal kindly with others is to deal with them as your own kin. After all, other believers are your brethren in the Lord. All the King's men actively look for opportunities to show kindness. Be like Jesus who practiced kindness that was considered radical for that time and culture. His kindness often extended to the people who were not treated well, including the sick, the poor, and the social outcasts. He healed them, fed them, and prayed for them. Sometimes it's the little things that count the most, even something small as a smile at a passing stranger. Interact with them instead of walking by looking down at the ground. That brief moment of kindness may be the only light someone sees all day.

Scripture reminds us that God delights in the mustard seed, the widow's mite, and the cup of cold water given in love. The kingdom is built not only through mighty works, but through consistent faithfulness in ordinary moments. Every kind word, every patient response, every compassionate glance becomes a thread God weaves into a much larger story. Don't underestimate the power of what feels small. When love motivates it, nothing is wasted. A smile, a word of encouragement, a moment of grace are sacred offerings. They may pass quickly from your awareness, but they can linger deeply in someone else's heart. In a world hungry for light, let God use your little things. They often count more than you'll ever know. Kindness is more than saying kind words. As a fruit of the Spirit it should stimulate you to loving actions toward others. It's true, actions do speak louder than words. James asks what good is it if you see a brother or sister naked and lacking daily food if you don't help them out (James 2:15,16).

Kindness that results in action is described by Jesus in His parable of the Good Samaritan. Luke 10:30-37 tells how a man was beaten by thieves, leaving him half dead. A certain priest and later a Levite came by, looked at the man, and passed by on the other side. Then a Samaritan man came by and had compassion on him. Samaritans were despised and considered unclean by the Jews yet here was one of them helping a man from Jerusalem who for certain despised him also. This Samaritan bandaged his wounds, set him on his own animal, brought him to an inn and took care of him. He did the right thing and Jesus said, "Go and do likewise" (vs. 37). This parable was told by Jesus to show what it means to love your neighbor as yourself. It reveals that love and kindness are not real unless actions are involved. The verbs "go" and "do" are commands to make the demonstration of mercy and kindness a lifestyle, something all the King's men should practice for the rest of their lives.

The sixth fruit of the Spirit is goodness. The Greek word "agathosune" is defined as 'virtue equipped at every point; uprightness of heart and life.' Kindness and goodness are similar in nature yet are not identical. Goodness involves being kind but it includes an additional aspect of honesty and firmness when relating to others. Kindness is a quality that causes you to act toward others in a kindly manner whereas goodness might and could rebuke and discipline others for what they do. Goodness is not afraid to confront what is wrong. It may rebuke, correct, or discipline - not to wound, but to heal; not to shame, but to restore. Where kindness soothes, goodness strengthens. Where kindness embraces, goodness redirects. A kind heart without goodness may tolerate what harms. A good heart without kindness may speak truth without grace. But when kindness and goodness walk together, they reflect the very nature of God who is merciful yet holy, gentle yet just.

Kindness is when you care about people; goodness is when you care enough about them to tell them the truth. True spiritual maturity learns when to extend kindness and when to exercise goodness. One comforts the broken; the other corrects the wayward. Both are acts of love, and both are necessary. Love that never corrects may feel gentle, but it can quietly abandon a soul to confusion. When love refuses to speak truth, it allows harmful paths to remain unchallenged. True love cares too deeply to watch someone drift without direction, and it speaks not to control, but to guide toward life, wholeness, and freedom. Yet correction without kindness carries its own danger. Words spoken without compassion may be true, but they can land like stones instead of healing balm. Truth delivered harshly can wound the heart, harden the spirit, and push people farther from the very change that correction seeks to produce. Correction that lacks love may win an argument, but it often loses a person.

God's way is neither permissive silence nor harsh rebuke. It is truth wrapped in grace. Divine love corrects because it sees value worth preserving, and divine kindness speaks because it desires restoration, not humiliation. In this balance, correction becomes an act of mercy, and kindness becomes a vessel for truth. When love and correction walk together, the soul is guided without being crushed, and the heart is healed without being deceived. This is the way of Christ - firm in truth, rich in mercy, leading not to shame, but to transformation. May all the King's men grow in discernment, having eyes to see beyond the surface and hearts tuned to the quiet voice of truth. May they walk in kindness with compassion, not as weakness, but as the strength that heals wounds and lifts the fallen. May they stand in goodness with courage, choosing what is right even when it is costly, and holding fast to righteousness when the path is narrow. May love be the motive and restoration be the goal.

Let their lives reflect the heart of the King they serve - firm yet gentle, bold yet humble, unwavering yet merciful - so that wherever they go, light overcomes darkness, grace triumphs over judgment, and the kingdom of God is made visible through them. Eph. 5:9 (TPT) says, "And the supernatural fruits of His light will be seen in you - goodness, righteousness, and truth." We see here that goodness is related to righteousness. You are righteous and you have righteous standards that can make you serious in your convictions. You know what is right and you expect others to do what is right. Sometimes it will be necessary to say difficult things for the other person's benefit. When Jesus dealt firmly with people it was not because

He ran out of patience with them. No, He spoke sternly and honestly with people as an act of kindness and love with the ultimate motive of doing good, both to them and to others who heard Him. Jesus did not always speak softly, but He always spoke lovingly.

His words were never careless, never cruel, and never driven by pride. When He spoke sternly, it was not to wound but to heal; not to condemn, but to awaken. On one occasion Jesus admonished Martha, one of His closest friends, when she rebuked her sister Mary for listening to Jesus instead of helping to prepare the meal for their quests. Another time He was more stern when He drove the money changers out of the temple. This also was an act of goodness for it upheld the righteous standard He lived by. He confronted hypocrisy because unchecked hypocrisy poisons both the heart that harbors it and the community that witnesses it. He rebuked pride because pride blinds people to their need for God. He spoke plainly about sin because silence would have been unkind. To allow deception to persist would have been to abandon people to destruction. His firmness was not the absence of love - it was love strong enough to risk misunderstanding for the sake of redemption.

Jesus understood that kindness is not always gentle in tone, but it is always good in purpose. A surgeon's scalpel may cut, yet it saves a life. In the same way, Christ's honest words cut through self-deception so that truth could bring freedom. Every correction carried an invitation. Every rebuke held out a path to restoration. And His words were not only for the one being addressed. They were spoken for the sake of all who listened. When Jesus corrected one heart publicly, He protected many others quietly. His truth established boundaries, clarified right-eousness, and set a standard of life that would guide genera-tions. Love, for Him, was never limited to the moment - it looked forward to the good that truth would produce in many lives. In Jesus we learn that love does not avoid hard conver-sations. Love tells the truth with courage. Love speaks clearly when eternity is at stake. And love always aims at what is good for the individual, good for the community, and good for the glory of God.

People in the kingdom of God need goodness which at one and the same time can be both kind and strong. The fruit of goodness leads people toward reform and change. Rom. 15:14 (TPT), "I am fully convinced of your genuine spirituality. I know each of you are stuffed full of goodness and that you are empowered to effectively instruct one another." The fruit of goodness helps you to speak the truth in love (Eph. 4:15) without bashing people over the head because they missed the mark. This is the kindly side of your convictions. All the King's men are to have a great love for the truth of God's Word and they're to share it with others in the right spirit, in a way that others will receive what they're saying. Scottish minister William Blaikie said, "Good tidings spoken harshly are not good tidings. The charm of the message is destroyed by the cruel spirit of the messenger." Love always seeks the highest good in the one loved. It speaks the truth to lead the person away from error and into a more rewarding life.

Through the spirit of goodness, you'll be able to impart a blessing to others as you help them to mature and develop in every area of their life to become more like Christ. True love will always speak at the right time, with the right words, and with the right spirit of goodness. This way no one will take offense when you speak to them. You can be fearless in standing for the truth and still be gentle and kind. Truth declared in a contentious manner will neither preserve unity nor promote usefulness. Pastor and author Lehman Strauss said, "It is not enough that our tongues hold to the truth; the truth must hold our tongues in love." John Stott said, "Truth becomes hard if it is not softened by love and love becomes soft if it is not strengthened by the truth." The fruit of goodness holds the two together. A man operating in the fruit of goodness cares about the moral well-being of others. His only aim is to do what is good and helpful to solidify the quality of one's moral worth.

Goodness is moral and spiritual excellence manifested in active kindness. It's a virtue characterized especially by interest in the welfare of others. It is the generosity which springs from the heart that is kind and will always take care to obtain for others that which is useful and beneficial. Paul said in 1 Thess. 5:15, "See that no one repays another evil for evil, but always seek after that which is good for one another and for all people." The Greek word for "seek" is "dioko" and it means 'to press hard after; to pursue with earnestness and diligence in order to obtain; to hunt, pursue, seek eagerly.' Always keep looking for ways to help make the lives of other people better. Rom. 14:19 says, "So let us pursue the things which make for peace and the building up of one another." Goodness doesn't tear down, it builds up. It does whatever is useful and helpful and beneficial as it eagerly seeks to strengthen those who need it most.

Eph. 4:19, "Let no corrupt communication proceed out of your mouth, but that which is good for necessary edification that it may impart grace to the hearers." Yes, you are to confront lapses in moral behavior but never let hateful words come out of your mouth. Instead, let your words become beautiful gifts that encourage others. AMP, "Use only such speech as is good and beneficial to the spiritual progress of others, as is fitting to the need and the occasion that it may be a blessing and give grace to those who hear it." Don't say anything that would tear down or hurt another person. Speak only what is good and edifying so that you can give help whenever and wherever it is needed. Prov. 12:18 says, "The tongue of the wise brings healing." Your harvest, that which you wish to accomplish, all depends on the manner in which you sow your words. Prov. 15:23 says, "A word spoken in due season, how good it is." Prov. 16:24, "Pleasant words are like a honeycomb, sweetness to the soul and health to the bones."

Good, wholesome words are gracious and tender and are sensitive to the needs of others. They show love to others the way Jesus showed compassion to the woman caught in adultery. Walk in the fruit of goodness and out of your innermost being good, healthy words suited for the occasion will flow out of you like rivers of living water (John 7:38). Your words of edification should always fit the occasion. Speak to them in such a way as to help them exactly where they are in order to get them where they're supposed to be. Use wisdom when you speak to others. "Let your speech always be with grace, as though seasoned with salt, so that you will know how you should respond to each person" (Col. 4:6). Job was paid a tremendous compliment in Job 4:4, "Your words have upheld him who was stumbling, and you have strengthened the feeble knees." Job's words helped others who were struggling. Such are the words that all the King's men should be speaking. With the fruit of goodness, they can do just that.

# | 8 |

# "THE FRUIT OF THE SPIRIT-PART 4"

The seventh fruit of the Spirit is faithfulness. The Greek word "Pistis" refers to that virtue which makes a person one on whom others can rely on. It describes one's trustworthiness, loyalty, reliability, constancy, and dependability. The man with this quality keeps his word, his promises, and his vows. A man who is faithful walks in integrity at all times - not only when eyes are watching, but especially when they are not. His character does not shift with convenience or pressure. What he is in private matches what he professes in public, because truth has taken root in his heart He can be trusted because honesty governs his words and actions. He does not bend the truth to protect himself, nor does he compromise what is right to gain favor or advantage. His "yes" means yes, and his "no" is anchored in conviction, not fear. Steadfast and dependable, he stands firm when others waver, choosing faithfulness over popularity and righteousness over reward.

This man is unwavering in loyalty - not to opinions or trends, but to what is true, right, and good. He honors God with his decisions, people with his conduct, and life with his consistency. Integrity is his covering, faithfulness his testimony, and trust his legacy. Such a man becomes a quiet strength in a noisy world, a living witness that faithfulness still matters and that truth, when walked out daily, carries its own reward. Faithfulness is an attribute of God. Ps. 36:5 says, "The faithfulness of God reaches to the clouds." Oh yes, so wonderfully great is the faithfulness of God. Lam. 3:23 says, "The steadfast love of the Lord never ceases; His mercies never come to an end. They are new every morning; Great is Your faithfulness." Faithfulness is not optional for those who belong to the King. It is not a personality trait, a spiritual gift, or a convenient choice - it is a calling. Since God is faithful, all the King's men must be faithful also. 1 John 4:14 says, "For as He is, even so are we in this world."

God has never failed to keep His word. From generation to generation, He has proven Himself steady, trustworthy, and unchanging. His faithfulness is not dependent on our performance; it flows from His nature. He is faithful because He is faithful. And because we serve a faithful King, His servants must reflect His character. All the King's men represent Him wherever they go. Their conduct speaks of His rule. Their loyalty reflects His honor. The faithfulness of all men is meant to testify to the faithfulness of God Himself. When they are steady, dependable, and obedient - especially when it is difficult - they proclaim to the world that their King is worthy of trust. Faithfulness is proven in the unseen places. It is shown in private obedience, not public applause. It is revealed when the path is long, the reward delayed, and the battle weary. Anyone can start strong, but it takes a faithful heart to finish well. God does not call His men to be impressive - He calls them to be faithful.

When God is your King, you will be faithful in prayer, faithful in integrity, faithful in marriage, faithful in service, faithful when no one is watching and faithful when the cost is high. The King has been faithful to us through our failures, our wandering, and our weakness. He has kept covenant when we broke it. He has stood firm when we faltered. And now, as men under His rule, we are called to stand firm for Him. Being faithful is commanded of all men. 1 Cor. 4:2 says, "It's required of stewards that a man be found faithful." Reliability is a trait we must all have. So important is this fruit of the Spirit that when the Lord returns the only absolute requirement by which He will judge His servants is faithfulness (Matt. 24:45,46). Were they true to what He commanded them to do? God supplies all we need: His Word, His Spirit, His gifts, His power. All we give is our faithfulness in using these resources. God will judge His stewards on how faithful they were and not on how much success they achieved.

In order to be faithful, you must be steadfast in your affections for and your allegiance to God. You must be dependable and unswerving in your loyalty to Him. Webster's dictionary says "faithful" means 'firm in adherence to whatever one owes allegiance, whether it be a person or thing or promise by which a tie was contracted.' To be a good steward, there must be an abandonment of oneself. Only those who are yielded to the cause of Christ will voluntarily surrender their will to His will. Jesus was faithful in His voluntary surrender to death on the cross in obedience to the Father's will and plan. The faithfulness of Christ is to be mirrored by all the King's men. God is faithful to His people, and He expects them to be faithful to Him. If you'll remain loyal to your commitments, your faithfulness will greatly influence how you love God and others. In the teachings of Jesus throughout the four gospels faithfulness is a recurring theme, emphasized through parables and direct exhortations to His disciples.

The parable of the talents (Matt. 25:14-30) and of the faithful servant (Luke 12:25-40) illustrates the importance of steadfast commitment and reliability is our actions and relationships. The virtue of faithfulness embodies unwavering commitment, steadfast loyalty, and trustworthiness in our interactions with God and those around us. True faithfulness encompasses a deep-rooted fidelity that enriches both our spiritual lives and our relationships with those around us. It's an active demonstration of loyalty and trustworthiness. Charles Spurgeon said this about faithfulness, "Reliability, keeping good faith with others, so that they know that your word is as good as your bond." Faithfulness describes the kind of person we should all aspire to be, to be a faithful friend in whom others can confide in, one whose loyalty they can rely on. Be a friend whose actions reflect an unwavering desire to promote the well-being of others. A life characterized by faithfulness can be a source of great comfort and strength.

As you strive to cultivate this fruit of the Spirit, may you find joy in building relationships founded on the rock of trust, loyalty, and unyielding devotion. Prov. 12:22 says, "Those who deal faithfully are His delight." It honors God and pleases Him when He knows you will faithfully carry out His divine will for your life. True faithfulness is when the faithfulness of God is imputed into your inner man by the power of the Holy Spirit. Like Him, let it be said of you, "Great is your faithfulness." All the King's men are to be faithful to their word and their promises. They walk in such a way that they are men who can be trusted to do what they say they are going to do. They are faithful to their calling and always manifest dependability in the discharge of the responsibilities which the Lord sees fit to lay upon them. 1 Sam. 26:23 says, "The Lord will repay each man for his righteousness and his faithfulness." The goal of every man should be to hear the Lord say, "Well done, good and faithful servant" (Matt. 25:23).

The eighth fruit of the spirit is gentleness. The Greek word "prautes" is defined as 'meekness; restrained power; patient trust in the midst of difficult circumstances.' Jesus gave us the perfect picture of gentleness in Matt. 21:5, "See, your King comes to you, gentle and riding on a donkey." He now offers us His gentleness as a gift. To be gentle means to be polite and have restrained behavior toward others. It takes a strong man to be truly gentle. It's when you place your strength under God's guidance. To be gentle is not to be weak, timid, or silent - it is to be polite in spirit and restrained in response. Gentleness chooses grace over harshness, patience over impulse, and humility over the need to dominate. It is strength under control. A gentle person knows how to speak without crushing, correct without condemning, and stand firm without being abrasive. Gentleness listens before it reacts. It considers the weight of words before releasing them.

True gentleness understands that people are often fighting unseen battles and therefore handles others with care. Spirit-led tenderness is guided by love. It does not excuse wrongdoing, but it confronts it with wisdom. It does not surrender truth, but it delivers truth in a way that invites healing rather than resistance. Gentleness is the posture of a heart that trusts God enough to remain calm, respectful, and steady even when provoked. In a loud, aggressive world, gentleness stands out. It reflects the character of Christ, who was firm in conviction yet tender with people. To be gentle is to let your strength serve others rather than intimidate them showing that maturity is not found in force, but in restraint. Gentleness constrains and channels the power of God at work inside us. We are able to correct others with easiness instead of arguing in resentment and rage. Paul said in Gal. 6:1, "If anyone is caught in a trespass, you who are spiritual restore such a one in a spirit of gentleness."

As the old saying goes, you catch more flies with honey than vinegar. Titus 3:2 says, "They must not slander anyone and must avoid quarreling. Instead, they should be gentle and show true humility to everyone." The Passion Translation says, "And remind them to never tear down anyone with their words or quarrel, but instead be considerate, humble, and courteous to everyone." C. Norman Bartlett said, "Steam does the most work when it makes the least noise. We do well to store up the capital of quietude against the day of need." Paul asked, "Shall I come to you with a rod, or with love and a spirit of gentleness?" (1 Cor. 4:21). In other words, things need not shatter in order to matter. Correction does not always require severity, and authority does not always need force to be effective. Paul made it clear that while discipline has its place, his deepest desire was to approach them in love, not to break them, but to build them. Transformation is measured by how deeply the heart is reached.

A gentle word, spoken in truth, can accomplish what a heavy hand never will. Love has a way of disarming pride, opening ears, and inviting repentance without humiliation. The rod represents authority used to restrain, but gentleness represents authority used to restore. One corrects behavior; the other reshapes character. God often prefers the latter not because He lacks power, but because He values relationship. His goal is not to crush us into submission, but to draw us into maturity. When love leads and gentleness guides, hearts are strengthened, faith grows deeper, and obedience becomes willing rather than forced. Jesus said in Matt. 11:29 (TPT), "Simply join your life with Mine. Learn My ways and you'll discover that I'm gentle, humble, easy to please. You will find refreshment and rest in Me." All the King's men are not easily provoked but are gentle and tender as Christ was. They're able to provide a soothing influence on someone who is resentful toward life.

The Greek word "prautes" means to have a gentle strength. It was a word used to describe a soothing wind, a healing medicine, and a horse that had been broken. It is power under control, strength under submission. Just as wisdom is the right use of knowledge, so gentleness is the right use of authority and power. A man who is gentle has his feelings and emotions under perfect control. Gentleness is an internal posture, a positioning of the heart, a bowing of your knee. God chooses gentleness to represent His greatness. He used the gentleness of a shepherd boy to take on the greatness of a giant, the meekness of Moses to confront a prideful Pharaoh. The evidence of gentleness is a deliberate placing of oneself under divine authority. It's when you place your mind under the authority of God to let Him control it. Scottish theologian William Barclay says "prautes" is "the watchdog who is bravely hostile to strangers and gently friendly with familiars whom he knows and loves."

Gentleness is having sensitivity for another person. It is concerned for their welfare, safety, and security. It is grounded in humility and is free of all roughness and abrasiveness. You must be intentionally kind and mild-mannered toward others. It stands to reason that a Spirit-led man is the one most suited to help people with a spirit of gentleness. Maintaining a gentle spirit is a sure sign of strength. Jesus was a gentle man wherever He went but He was not quiet, and He certainly was not a push over. Decide to be gentle in everything you say and do. 2 Sam. 22:36 says, "You have given me the shield of Your salvation, and Your gentleness has made me great." Paul emphasized the importance of gentleness and its powerful and transformative quality, urging believers to "let your gentleness be known to all men" (Phil. 4:5). Have a reputation for being gentle. Let your unselfish meekness be recognized by all people. Extend to others the kindly consideration you would wish to receive yourself.

Kenneth Wuest said, "Do not keep the sweet gentleness in your heart. Let it find expression in your conduct. Thus others will experience its blessings also." Jesus embodied the virtue of gentleness when He healed the sick, fed the hungry, and forgave sinners. He always demonstrated love and gentleness with those He encountered. Likewise, when you show gentleness toward others, you are showing them love and respect while at the same time creating an environment of safety and trust. Gentleness is an important virtue to cultivate in your life. It's what causes you to become an agent of God's love and compassion to the world you live in. Gentleness can bring healing, reconciliation, and peace to those around you. It puts others first and extends grace, love, and kindness even to those who are difficult to like. Ask God to bring circumstances into your life that allow you to practice tenderness and meekness to others. For sure, being gentle can make all the difference in your part of the world.

The ninth fruit of the Spirit is self-control. The Greek word "egkrateia" describes the mastery over fleshly impulses, the ability to take a grip of oneself. It refers to the restraining of passions and appetites that originate from your old sinful nature. No longer are you to live in bondage to the desires of the flesh. This virtue is very important to your walk as a man.

Prov. 25:28 says, "Whoever has no rule over his own spirit is like a city whose walls are broken down." In the ancient world, a city without walls was exposed, vulnerable, and destined for defeat. Walls were not a sign of pride, but of wisdom. They defined what was allowed in and what was kept out. In the same way, self-control is the wall around the soul. When you fail to govern your spirit - your emotions, reactions, desires, and words - you leave your inner life open to invasion. Anger storms in unchecked. Fear occupies territory it was never meant to claim. Temptation enters freely, not because it is strong, but because there is no resistance.

God does not call us to be emotionless, but to be governed. Strength is not found in giving full expression to every feeling, but in submitting those feelings to truth. A ruled spirit listens before reacting, prays before speaking, and waits before acting. It understands that restraint is not weakness - it is wisdom in action. When the walls are rebuilt through prayer, discipline, and dependence on the Spirit, peace is restored. The city becomes secure again. The enemy may still shout from the outside, but he no longer has free access within. Rule your spirit, and you protect what God has entrusted to you. Guard the walls, and your life becomes a place where righteousness dwells and God's peace reigns. If you live without restraint, if your passions and desires go outside the will of God, you're as helpless as a city with no walls that is open to the attacks of the enemy. A ruled spirit does not surrender control - it submits it to God. And in that surrender, it becomes unshakable.

Prov. 16:32 says, "He who rules his spirit is better than he who takes a city." Having self-control is key to being useful in the kingdom of God. This is why you are to keep your body and its fleshly desires in complete subjection to your spirit. 1 Peter 2:11,12 says, "Abstain from fleshly lusts which war against the soul. Be careful to live properly among the Gentiles." The Passion Translation says, "Divorce yourselves from evil." Gal. 5:24,25 says, "And they that are Christ's have crucified the flesh with its passions and desires. If we live in the Spirit, let us also walk in the Spirit." If your sensual appetites are out of control, then you must do what Paul did, "I beat my body and bring it under submission" (1 Cor. 9:27). Paul is not promoting self-harm; he is describing spiritual discipline. You must bring your body under control. Paul is saying to beat your inward passions and lusts. W. E. Vine says this is "not the bruising of the body itself, but rigid self-denial in order to keep oneself spiritually fit."

Left unchecked, the body wants comfort over calling, pleasure over purpose, ease over obedience. The flesh tells you to do what feels good, but the Spirit calls you to something higher. Spiritual maturity is reached when the will submits to God, even when the body resists. Paul uses athletic language because athletes understand discipline. No runner wins a race by indulging every appetite. No boxer lands decisive blows by swinging wildly. Victory requires restraint, focus, and training. To "beat the body" means to deny its right to be in charge. It means fasting when the body demands food, praying when it demands sleep, obeying when it demands comfort, and standing firm when it demands escape. It is the daily choice to crucify the flesh and submit to the Spirit. This discipline is not about earning God's favor - it is about protecting your calling. Paul feared being disqualified, not because salvation is fragile, but because influence, effectiveness, and usefulness can be lost when self-control is abandoned.

Submission is not weakness - it is strength under control. When the body is trained instead of indulged, the spirit becomes sharp, the conscience becomes clear, and the life becomes fruitful. God does not call us to pamper the flesh, but to master it. The fruit of self-control speaks of being controlled by an inner strength which ultimately is the power of the Holy Spirit. This self-denial is literally Spirit-enabled self-denial. Having self-control and self-discipline is serious business. With the Holy Spirit inside of you, you'll have the power and ability to control your thoughts, words, and actions. Paul said in Rom. 6:6, "Our old self was crucified with Him so that the body of sin might be done away with, that we should no longer be slaves to sin." Jesus died to dismantle the stronghold of sin so that you would not continue to live one moment longer submitted to sin's power. As the Spirit gives you self-control, you can refuse to sin.

Aristotle once said, "I count him braver who overcomes his desires than him who conquers his enemies; for the hardest victory is the victory over self." Prov. 16:32 says this about self-control, "He who is slow to anger is better than the mighty, and he who rules his spirit than he who captures a city." All the King's men are motivated to be the man God created them to be. To achieve this goal, they must resist the distractions that originate from their fleshly passions and desires. Self-control is the virtue that makes you fit to be the servant of others. Before you can lead others down the right path, you must first go down that right path yourself. How do you do that? By taking control of your sinful nature. Having victory over the flesh comes when you do your part as you rely on the enabling power of the Holy Spirit. You must continually bring your body under subjection. Moment by moment, hour by hour, and day by day you must deny your body the right to do what it wants to do.

You must literally bring your body into a state of servitude, to make it a slave, to bring it into a state of subjection. You control your body, don't let your body control you. When Joseph came face-to-face with his brothers who sold him into slavery, he masterfully controlled his emotions as he sought to love, forgive, and provide for them in their time of need. On the other hand, consider the sad story of Samson and his self-destruction and defeat at the hands of the seductive Delilah. His life ended early because of a lack of self-control. What is self-control? It's the power of God inside of you that helps you do what you want to do and not do what you shouldn't do so that you can have a good life in the future. Self-control and self-discipline are two sides of the same coin. Both are needed. Self-control restrains our negative impulses, and self-discipline takes positive action. Prov. 4:23 says, "Watch over your heart with all diligence for from it flow the springs of life."

Above all else, guard your heart for it affects everything you do. The Passion Translation says, "Pay attention to the welfare of your inner most being for from there flows the wellspring of life." To have self-control, you must live from the inside out. If you've sinned and missed the mark because of a lack of self-control, then repent as quickly as you can "so that times of refreshing may come from the presence of the Lord" (Acts 3:19). Col. 1:10 says "to walk worthy of the Lord, fully pleasing Him, being fruitful in every good work." Do that and you'll be "strengthened with all might according to His glorious power" (vs. 11). It's God's power working in you that causes you to attain steadfastness and endurance, to gain dominance over all fleshly desires, to daily walk in the fruit of self-control. Because God has given you new life in Christ and His Holy Spirit to dwell in you, you have both the responsibility and the ability to yield your self-will to His revealed will. That is self-control.

# | 9 |

# "CHARACTER FROM ABOVE"

In the kingdom of God, character matters. To be a real man doesn't mean you have to hunt and fish and ride motorcycles and work on cars and chop your own firewood. What makes a man a real man is not found in his skills, his abilities, or his hobbies. These things may impress others, but they do not define the true measure of a man. Strength, talent, and achievement can be developed, displayed, and even lost but character is revealed from the inside out. A real man is shaped by his inward character. It is the unseen part of him - the heart, the conscience, the spirit - that carries the greatest weight. This is the part of a man that God formed with eternal purpose, creating him in the image of Christ. While the world celebrates performance, God looks at the heart. The character of Christ within a man is what gives him true strength. It produces humility instead of pride, integrity instead of compromise, courage instead of fear, and love instead of selfish ambition.

When a man is conformed to Christ, his life reflects patience under pressure, faithfulness when no one is watching, and obedience even when it costs him something. Skills can build careers, and abilities can open doors, but Christlike character builds lives, families, and legacies. A man who walks in the image of Christ becomes a steady foundation - someone others can trust, follow, and lean on. His words carry weight because his life carries truth. In the end, a real man is not defined by what he can do with his hands, but by who he has become in his heart. God has never been impressed by ability without integrity. He does not measure a man by his resume, his muscles, or his accomplishments, but by his humility, his obedience, and his willingness to be transformed. The world celebrates what a man can do. God examines who a man is. When Christ is formed within him, everything else falls into its proper place. This is the mark of true manhood - not outward display, but inward transformation.

Paul gave us a picture of godly character when he exhorted all men in 1 Cor. 16:13 to "be watchful, stand firm in the faith, act like men, be strong." These four exhortations have a military tone to them. All the King's men must be as sentinels on guard, must maintain their position, must manifest courage, and must become strong. All real men are firm in defending their faith and maintaining their integrity. They act in a valiant and courageous way and run toward the giants who stand before them. All these qualities are masculine, and Paul is saying that to develop the character of a real man these commands must be put into practice immediately and lived out continually. Conduct is the offspring of character. Conduct is eternal, character is internal. Conduct is what we do, character is what we are. Character is the root of the tree; good conduct is the fruit it bears. A man with character faithfully follows God's Word each and every day. His authority is established, and he's got his marching orders.

A real man protects those under his care. He excels in the work he's been given to do. He makes this world a better place. He fulfills his God-given destiny. David told his son Solomon just before he died, "Be strong and prove yourself a man" (1 Kings 2:2). In other words, be a man with godly character. Be a man's man. As the excellence of gold is its purity, so the excellence of man is his character. Men of character are known for their honesty, their moral ethics, and their charity. 2 Peter 1:5-8 says faith, virtue, knowledge, self-control, steadfastness, godliness, brotherly kindness, and love are the traits of a man with character. He is honest, displays moral excellence, and has a good reputation. He desires to do right and will accept responsibility. He is Christlike and always follows the example of Jesus. John Maxwell once said, "We teach what we know, but we reproduce who we are." The truth be told, your character is on display whether you know it or not.

Long before a word is spoken, your life is already preaching. Your reactions, your choices, your tone, and your consistency quietly reveal what truly lives in your heart. Character is not proven in public moments - it is revealed in private ones. It shows up when no one is watching, when pressure is heavy, when the outcome is uncertain, and when doing right costs you something. Titles, gifts, and talents may impress people for a season, but character determines whether your influence lasts. 1 Samuel 16:7 says, "Man looks at the outward appearance, but the Lord looks at the heart." God sees beyond the polished exterior and examines the motives beneath the surface. What we hide from others is never hidden from Him. And often, what we try to conceal eventually speaks for itself. Your character is on display in how you treat people who can do nothing for you. It is seen in how you respond to correction, how you handle disappointment, and how you conduct yourself when things do not go your way.

Men of character will set a good example for others to follow, and their godly reputation will be evident to all (Titus 2:7,8). It's your character that shows who rules your heart. Christian character is shaped when you surrender to God's plan and purpose for your life. You will grow and be enriched as you learn to model Christ in everything you do. Your character summarizes the essence of your walk with Christ which is exhibited back to Him and then to others. It shows others that you are one of the King's men. When you are faced with the challenges of life and choose to respond in a godly manner, you develop character. Your actions become your habits, and your habits become your character. Andy Stanley said, "Your character reaches into every facet of your life. It is more far-reaching than your talent, your education, your background, or your network of friends. Those things can open doors for you, but your character will determine what happens once you pass through those doors."

Paul left Titus in Crete to get the church in order (Titus 1:5). The greatest need in that highly dysfunctional church was godly men who displayed character in their lives. The church had men, but not the right kind. It was filled with idle talkers and deceivers, lazy gluttons, men who were detestable, disobedient, unfit for any good work (vs. 10-16). When Paul told Titus to look for men to lead the church, he did not tell him to look for intelligence, talent, or popularity. He told him to look for men with strong character. Titus 1:7 says a man with character must be blameless and above reproach. This is the one quality every man must cultivate for all other virtues flow from this one. To be blameless means you are a man of unquestionable integrity. You are a man in whom no criticism can be found. You are a man who is worthy material for others to follow. It does not mean to be perfect; it means to be whole. It is the mark of a man whose life is aligned, whose private conduct matches his public confession.

In a world crowded with compromise, the blameless man stands firm. He understands that integrity is not built in moments of ease but proven in seasons of pressure. He chooses righteousness when no one is watching and faithfulness when it costs him something. Titus 1:8 says you must be self-controlled and live a disciplined life without which you will be arrogant, quick-tempered, a drunkard, violent, and greedy for gain (vs. 7). Titus 2:6 says, "Likewise, urge the young men to be self-controlled." You need to learn to control your flesh when you are young. If you don't, it will control you when you get older. Being a man of character and doing what God has called you to do demands courage. Why? Because serving God is not easy. Every assignment He gives you will be hard to fulfill. God's calling in your life demands courage and one of the greatest tools of the enemy is to get you to be passive. As you walk with the Lord, you will grow both in character and in courage.

You will grow in your ability to discern when courage is needed. You will develop the depth of character that is needed to do what is right no matter what the cost may be. Don't pray for an easy life, pray to be a stronger man. It's not doing easy things that lead to greatness, it's doing the hard things with the strength in you that no one else wants to do. Pastor Josh Smith said, "If a man is not willing to do the hard things, make the hard decisions, and suffer for what is right, everyone around him suffers." Be bold and strong and steadfast and do not fear those who rise against you. Act like a man and be strengthened in your confidence that "if God be for you, who can be against you?" (Rom. 8:31). There is no limit to what a man with character can do. The sky truly is the limit when the standard he sets for his life lines up with the revealed will of God. God's character must become your character, and this won't happen on its own. You must apply great diligence to the cultivation of godly character.

For sure, godly character does not develop by accident. It is not the result of good intentions, momentary inspiration, or occasional spiritual effort. It is cultivated slowly, intentionally, and with great diligence. Just as a farmer cannot expect a harvest without preparing the soil, planting seed, and tending the field, no believer can expect strong character without disciplined spiritual labor. We are called to "give all diligence to add to our faith virtue, knowledge, self-control, perseverance, godliness, brotherly kindness, and love" (2 Peter 1:5-7). These qualities do not appear overnight. They are forged through consistent obedience, daily submission, and a deliberate pursuit of righteousness. Diligence means you guard your thoughts, discipline your desires, and align your actions with God's Word even when it is inconvenient. It is the refusal to settle for spiritual mediocrity. When character is cultivated with diligence, faith becomes visible, integrity becomes evident, and Christ is glorified.

Make no mistake about it, a man's character is what makes him a man. It is the foundation of manhood. Build it daily through prayer, obedience, and perseverance. For when everything else fades, a godly character will stand, and through it, a man will leave a legacy that honors God and blesses generations to come. In the same way a man works hard to provide for his family, even more so he should work hard to be a man of character. You were born a male, but you must grow into a man. The cultivation of character must become a constant, compelling, and lifelong commitment. If you neglect the pursuit of godly character, everything else in your life will crumble. And remember, the goal is not to be a good man, the goal is to be a godly man. The utmost goal of your life is to manifest the life of Jesus to those around you. Seek to trust and follow Him every day making the character of Jesus your greatest pursuit. You must cultivate your inner man because inside of you is the man you really are.

Heb. 1:3 says Jesus was the "express image" of God the Father. The Greek word used here is "charakter" and this is the only place in scripture this word is found. This is where the word "character" comes from and it means 'to engrave; to mark; to imprint.' This is saying the imprint we leave on people's lives define what our character is. To have godly character is to be like Jesus who scripture says "is the dazzling radiance of God's splendor, the exact expression of God's true nature - His mirror image!" (TPT). A man with character is upright and walks in integrity at all times. He does the right thing over and over again until it becomes second nature to him. He does good and righteous things automatically. Building godly character doesn't passively happen. You don't become one of the King's men by accident. No, you must work hard and put forth much effort to cultivate godly virtues. Paul said you must "work out your own salvation with fear and trembling" (Phil. 2:12).

You must apply great diligence in order to become the man God wants you to be. Several people in the Bible are described as having noble character, people such as David (1 Sam. 13:14), Ruth (Ruth 3:11), Hanani (Neh. 7:2), and Job (Job. 2:3). Noah was also a man with character. Gen. 6:9 says, "Noah was a just man, perfect in his generations. Noah walked with God." He was a blameless man, a man of integrity. Noah had character because he was a just and righteous man. God said to him in Gen. 7:1, "I have seen that you are righteous before Me in this generation." The first step in building godly character is to get saved for this is how you become righteous. 2 Cor. 5:21 says Jesus died for us "that we might become the righteousness of God in Him." Once you're born again, the Holy Spirit can go to work inside of you. He will change you from the inside out as He develops Christlike character in your inner man. Godly character grows from this new identity.

You do not live righteously to become saved; you live righteously because you are saved. Phil. 1:6 (NLT) says, "And I am certain that God, who began the good work within you, will continue His work until it is finally finished on the day when Christ Jesus returns." It's faith in Christ that separates godly character from the way the world does things. It's the character from above that will help you be profitable, useful, and beneficial to others. God said of Job, "There is none like him on the earth, a blameless and upright man, one who fears God and shuns evil" (Job. 1:8). The NLT says, "He is the finest man in all the earth." Like Noah, Job was a man of great character and integrity. When attacked by Satan, vs. 20 says "he tore his robe and shaved his head, and he fell to the ground and worshipped." Job 2:3 goes on to say he "held fast to his integrity." In other words, he held fast to his character. He shunned evil and did not respond to his calamity in a sinful way.

Fearing God is what caused Job to depart from sin and live a perfect and upright life. Likewise, developing the fear of the Lord in your life will build in you a godly, Christlike character. This is not about terror or dread; it is about reverence, awe, and a deep respect for who God is. It is the settled awareness that God is holy, righteous, and worthy of your complete devotion. When this fear takes root in a believer's heart, it begins to shape character from the inside out. Developing the fear of the Lord teaches us to see life through God's eyes. It causes us to weigh our words, examine our motives, and choose obedience even when no one else is watching. This reverence restrains us from sin, not because we fear punishment, but because we do not want to grieve the heart of God. In this way, the fear of the Lord becomes a moral compass that keeps us aligned with truth. When you develop the fear of the Lord, you become marked by integrity, obedience, and a sincere desire to please God above all else.

Ultimately, the fear of the Lord builds a strong and godly character because it anchors your life in holiness and truth. It keeps your heart soft, your consciences tender, and your walk steady. As you learn to fear the Lord, you will grow into a man whose life clearly reflects the character of Christ bringing glory to God and light to the world. How do you learn to fear the Lord? First, you must choose to fear the Lord (Prov. 1:29). Choose to love what God loves and hate what God hates. Choose to read God's Word and apply it to your life. Prov. 2;1,2 says you are to "receive My words and treasure My commands within you. Incline your ear to wisdom and apply your heart to understanding." Vs. 4,5 says, "If you seek her as silver, and search for her as for hidden treasure, then you will understand the fear of the Lord and find the knowledge of God." To build godly character you must practice being in the presence of God. Invite Him into your daily life. Walk with Him and talk with Him all the time.

Be proactive in staying away from people, places, and situations that may lead you to sinful thinking and actions. If you play with fire, you almost certainly will be burned. Remind yourself that God is watching everything you think, say, and do. Prov. 15:3 says, "The eyes of the Lord are in every place, keeping watch on the evil and the good." God is all seeing and nothing escapes His notice. This is why you must ask Him daily to reveal to you where you're missing the mark and be quick to repent of it. Ps. 139:23,24 says, "Search me, O God, and know my heart; Try me, and know my thoughts; And see if there is any wicked way in me, and lead me in the way everlasting." Solomon said in Eccl. 12:13 (TPT), "That's the whole story. Here now is my final conclusion: Fear God and obey His commands, for this is everyone's duty." Godly character does not come to you automatically. It is built on virtue, moral excellence, and spiritual energy. A strong effort must be made to become the man God wants you to be.

Daniel also was a man with a flawless character. In him was an "excellent spirit" (Dan. 6:3) because "he was faithful, nor was there any error or fault found in him" (vs. 4). He drew a line in the sand and would not do what the Babylonian culture dictated he should do. He refused to compromise the law of God that was written on his heart. Dan. 1:8 says he "purposed in his heart" not to sin against his God. Christian character is not forged in the moment of adversity, rather it is revealed in the moment of adversity. Daniel didn't become a man of character in Babylon where he was taken prisoner, he was a man of character before he got there. As a young man in Jerusalem, he learned to fear his God. For sure, character will not be developed without your involvement. Maximum effort must be put forth and there must be desire, determination, and discipline on your part. Like Daniel, you must exercise faith and apply all diligence to be a man with character.

Charles Spurgeon said, "God sends every bird his food but He doesn't throw it into the nest." The Greek word for "diligence" is "spoude" and it refers to 'eagerness, earnestness, willingness, and zeal.' It is a sign of quick movement or haste accompanying the eagerness. You should be eager to build godly character in your life. You should be forever ready to expend energy and effort to do those things that make you more like Christ. Character will not come if you sit still and do nothing. The word "spoude" speaks of intensity of purpose followed by intensity of effort toward the realization of that purpose. In other words, be in a hurry to develop godly character in your life. With divinely inspired swiftness be determined to live a life that is well pleasing to the Lord above. Take the initiative and begin to think and meditate on things that are virtuous, true, honorable, noble, pure and holy, merciful and kind, beautiful and respectful (Phil. 4:8).

Paul commands all men to carefully and continually focus on and fill their minds with all things that are virtuous and not just give them a fleeting thought. Reflect on and think about the things that bring about a godly character with a deep-seated determination to do them, to allow them to mold and shape your daily conduct. Meditate on godly virtues because noble thinking leads to noble living. This is why you need to continually think on these things in a detailed and logical manner. Prov. 23:7 says, "For as he thinks in his heart, so is he." This is saying that what you think about holds the key to the type of character you will have, whether good or bad. Take this seriously. Godly character and spiritual stability are a product of how you think. It is your responsibility, and yours alone, to determine what you think about. How you choose to think will affect what you say and what you do. It affects the type of man you will become. Always guard your mind and the things you think about.

David wrote in Ps. 19:14, "Let the words of my mouth and the meditation of my heart be acceptable in Your sight, O Lord, my strength and my redeemer." You can make a positive contribution to your character by controlling the things you think about for out of your heart "flow the issues of life" (Prov. 4:23). Fill your mind with scripture and focus on the Lord's commands and promises and goodness. Renew your mind (Rom. 12:2) so that you will think and act more like Jesus. Josh. 1:8, "This Book of the Law shall not depart from your mouth, but you shall meditate on it day and night, that you may observe to do according to all that is written in it." Meditation leads to action. This is why you should always "set your mind on things above, not on things on the earth" (Col. 3:2). The battle for godly character is in the way you think. Always ponder the things that will make you a better man. Fix your eyes on Jesus and the way He lived His life and then go out and do the same things He did.

# | 10 |

# "HOLY VIOLENCE"

Man was created to be God's representative on the earth and to live under His divine authority. The first gift God gave to man was dominion over all the earth (Gen. 1:26). David reaffirmed this vital truth when, speaking of man, he wrote in Ps. 8:6, "You have made him to have dominion over the works of Your hands; You have put all things under his feet." The word "dominion" means 'to rule; to dominate; to bring under control; to tread down; to prevail against.' From the very beginning, God entrusted the earth to man not as an owner but as a steward. This means that man was made to have mastery over everything God has made. Everything you touch - land, water, resources, creativity, strength, and wisdom - belongs first to Him. Your calling as one of the King's men is to manage what He has made in a way that reflects His heart. To be a steward is to serve. God placed Adam in the garden "to tend it and keep it" (Gen. 2:15), revealing that dominion was never meant to be domination, but responsibility.

Man was created to bring order from chaos, fruitfulness from potential, and blessing from what lies dormant. Every element of the earth carries purpose. Stewardship is the art of unlocking that purpose for good. When man works the soil, develops technology, cultivates knowledge, or builds communities, he is engaging in holy labor. True stewardship seeks the well-being of all mankind. The fields, forests, oceans, cities, and systems of this world are meant to bless generations, not be exhausted by greed. When you use what God has given to uplift life, protect dignity, and promote peace, you reflect His wisdom. To use creation to its full potential for good is to align your labor with God's purposes. It is to bring faith into action, love into leadership, and reverence into responsibility. A faithful steward understands that one day an account will be given not for how much was taken, but for how well it was used. Be a man who handles God's earth with care, courage, and vision

It is your responsibility to act as God would act so that His glory will spread to the ends of the earth. You're to bring every gift, resource, and opportunity into the service of God, for the flourishing of all people and the glory of His name. To take dominion means to take responsibility, to care, to cultivate, to lead. All the King's men are leaders who fully embrace the fact that they were created to dominate. As leaders they step forth and lead the charge into enemy territory. They're the ones who willfully sacrifice their life for others, the ones who absorb the impact. Jim Ramos said, "You're the man in the arena. You're the tip of the spear." Sam Roberts Jr. said, "The tip of a spear is the first to hit the target absorbing all the opposing energy and transferring what is left to the rest of the spear." Dan Fleming added, "When it hits the mark it opens up the path for the others to follow through! It makes a way!" These are the leaders the world is looking for.

A man who walks in dominion is the one out in front, gladly willing to sacrifice his life for others. The unofficial motto of the U. S. Coast Guard is, "You have to go out. You don't have to come back." Of the 1,514 people who died when the Titanic sank, 1,347 were men. On that boat were brave men willing to go down with the ship to save the lives of others. Strong men take dominion as they lead the way and pierce through the barriers before them. Their purpose is to help those they love to become the best version of themselves. Men who dominate are focused and stay sharp at all times. Abraham Lincoln once said, "If you give me six hours to cut down a tree, I'll spend the first four sharpening the ax." Strong men lead the way. Dominion is not about dominance over people, but responsibility before God. It is their calling to step forward when others hesitate, to stand firm when resistance rises, and to move with purpose when obstacles appear immovable.

A strong man understands that barriers are not signs to retreat, but invitations to advance. He pierces through fear, doubt, and opposition with faith and resolve. Where others see walls, he sees assignments. Where others see impossibility, he sees opportunity for God's strength to be revealed. True strength is anchored in obedience. A man who takes dominion first governs himself - his thoughts, his words, his passions, and his choices. From that inner mastery flows the courage to confront external challenges. He does not shrink back, complain, or wait for permission. He moves forward with wisdom, restraint, and conviction, knowing that God has entrusted him with ground to take. Strong men lead not by shouting from behind, but by walking ahead. They absorb the blows so others can advance. They break through resistance so those following can walk on cleared paths. Their leadership is sacrificial, their authority earned, and their direction clear.

To take dominion is to bring order where there is chaos, hope where there is despair, and light where darkness has ruled. Strong men rise, advance, and press through barriers not for their own glory, but to fulfill God's purpose and to make a way for others to follow. The Bible gives clarity on the meaning of dominion in Gen. 2:15 (ESV) which says, "The Lord God took the man and put him in the garden of Eden to work it and keep it." The primary role of every man is summarized in the words "work" and "keep." He is to sacrificially work hard for the sake of others and to keep watch over their physical, emotional, and spiritual well-being. Just as a plow is used to cultivate the earth, so are all the King's men to cultivate and nurture everything and everyone God has put under their care, to help them grow and thrive. Work is a call to cultivate God's world for His glory. Yes, working for others can sometimes be a selfless and thankless task but this is what every man has been called to do.

A real man lives an authentic life, fighting every day to be the best version of himself for others. He says, "Watch me. Follow my example and I'll take you all the way." Professor Robert Coleman said, "It is well enough to tell people what we mean, but it is infinitely better to show them how to do it. People are looking for demonstration, not explanation." All the King's men are called to rise up and take godly, loving, sacrificial dominion. It is their God-given duty to work hard, sweat, toil, and sacrifice for the good of others. Taking dominion is about manifesting the glory of God on the earth. Like throwing a huge stone into a pond, the ripple effect of what they do goes out to the ends of the earth. They're very observant and pay attention to what is going on around them. They survey what is happening in the lives of others and then prayerfully search for means to help them. It is their responsibility to lead people in the right direction, to take them from where they are to where God wants them to be.

All this, of course, takes a lot of sacrifice. They're like an offensive lineman in football who sacrifices his body so the guys with the ball can get all the glory. The sacrifices these linemen make often go unnoticed by those in the crowd. They do, however, live with the satisfaction that their sacrifice is what caused the team to win the game. Through the action of sacrifice, all the King's men die to their own desires so that others can have theirs. He lays down his life so others can have life more abundantly (John 10:10). The high call of strong men is to joyfully serve others, to gladly sacrifice his needs and desires for the happiness and well-being of those in his sphere of influence. Everybody wins when you decide to out-love and out-serve those you come in contact with. Weak men serve themselves but strong men, like Jesus, serve those they love. Be a man's man, a man who sacrifices for those he loves, a man who sheds blood, sweat, and tears to serve others.

Men who dominate are of great use in the kingdom of God. Every man can be a blessing to someone else as they yield to God so He can flow through them in a powerful way. Taking dominion is so important because it is needed each and every day. You need to understand that in life you are either going to dominate or be dominated. The choice is yours. Having dominion in your particular domain is part of your inheritance as a child of God. It's part of who you are in Christ. He restored back to man the dominion Adam lost in the garden. Every blessing that you are to have and enjoy flow from your inheritance to dominate. If you're not walking in dominion, you'll never be healthy, wealthy, and wise. You'll also never be able to be a blessing to other people. You dominate by pressing in to become the man God created you to be, by showing the devil who the real boss is. You don't float into the plan of God for your life. You fulfill your destiny by pressing in and taking dominion.

All the King's men are on fire to seize what belongs to them. Jesus said in Matt. 11:12, "And from the days of John the Baptist until now the kingdom of God suffers violence and the violent take it by force." That's dominion! The Passion Translation says, "The realm of heaven's kingdom is bursting forth, and passionate people have taken hold of its power." That's how you take dominion. You take hold of God's power. You dominate with holy violence, not with fists, weapons, or cruelty but with holy violence of the spirit. This is not a call to harm others, but a summons to aggressive faith, unyielding obedience, and the relentless pursuit of righteousness. Holy violence is the courage to confront sin within before correcting sin without. It is the forceful rejection of compromise, the tearing down of pride, lust, fear, and apathy. Godly men dominate when they take authority over their flesh, refuse to bow to weakness, and submit every thought, desire, and ambition to Christ.

This kind of dominance is forged in prayer, sharpened by discipline, and proven through obedience. It is the strength to say "no" to temptation and "yes" to sacrifice. Holy violence storms the gates of fear, presses through resistance, and refuses retreat when the cost is high. All the King's men lead the way by standing firm when others shrink back. They dominate darkness by walking in light, overpower deception with truth, and overcome evil with good. Their force is not destruction, but transformation. Their power is not control, but authority that comes from alignment with God. Holy violence builds homes, protects families, strengthens churches, and advances the Kingdom. It is love with backbone, faith with grit, and obedience with fire. This is how godly men dominate - not by breaking others, but by breaking through; not by conquering people, but by conquering self; not by earthly force, but by heaven's strength moving through a surrendered life.

Charles Spurgeon said, "The King sets forth the spirit demanded in those who would take part and lot in His great cause and kingdom. Lord, wake us up!" Amen to that. The term "take by force" is the Greek word "harpazo" and it means 'to take suddenly and vehemently, often with violence and speed or quickly and without warning.' To take dominion you must storm into the kingdom of heaven with great power and abruptness, rushing with eagerness to get in it with a violent zeal. With faith you're to take the kingdom of God by storm. What is faith? It's a living power from heaven which grasps and takes possession by force the promises of God. The devil many times will get the upper hand because men have never been violent in their battle against the forces of evil. You're to dominate the devil, not let the devil dominate you. Daily you must operate in your dominion. Violently speak to those demons and command them in the name of Jesus to get out of your life and the lives of your loved ones.

Victory is yours when you dominate! Stop praying sissy prayers, prayers that have no power behind them. The devil is under your feet so take your heel and crush his head. The devil does not rule - he trespasses. He operates only where believers fail to exercise their God-given authority. To walk in victory there must be a consistent exercise of dominion and authority. This must be your lifestyle if you are to move in the flow of what God is doing on the earth. Dominion must be exercised daily, not just when trouble raises its ugly head. Take dominion on good days when the sun is shining bright overhead. This can stop the storm clouds from rolling in. Dominion will put a hedge of protection around you that the enemy can't penetrate or break through. Be offensive in your fight with the devil. Attack him before he attacks you. Faith-filled words carry authority. Like an arrow shoot them at whatever circumstance you may be in. Take dominion. Resist the devil and watch him flee. He has no choice but to flee.

Take dominion. It is your responsibility to set in motion the direction your life will go. With extreme diligence on your part spiritual laws will operate fully and completely to make your life better. An all out effort will take you into your Promised Land. Those who don't dominate keep wandering around the same old mountain year after year after year. You can't be casual if your life is going in the wrong direction. Give it all you've got and God will sustain you and empower you and change your circumstances around. Momentum matters. Keep on keeping on! By taking dominion one victory quickly leads to another victory. You'll be like a huge stone rolling downhill where nothing can stop you. You need to renew your mind and consistently think on the right things. Let your thoughts work for you and not against you. Prov. 23:7 says, "For as a man thinks in his heart, so does he become." Take dominion and bring "every thought into captivity to the obedience of Christ" (2 Cor. 10:5).

The Message Bible says you are to "fit every loose thought into the structure of life shaped by Christ." You're in charge so capture every thought until it acknowledges the authority of Christ. You must rid your mind of everything that violates God's truth and God's will. Oswald Chambers said, "Be careful that you vigorously maintain God's perspective, and remember that it must be done every day, little by little. No outside power can touch the proper perspective." Your mind is the greatest gift God has given you and it must be devoted entirely to Him. Stop listening to the tyranny of unclean thoughts and bring freedom to your spiritual life. If you'll do that and start to speak faith-filled words, you'll take dominion and stop the devil in his tracks. When he sees God moving in your life, he'll move in the opposite direction. Take dominion and pray savage prayers. Use the Word of God to influence your circumstances. It was given to you as a seed to use in your time of need.

The Word of God will force things to happen in your life. Is. 55:11 says, "It shall accomplish what I please, and it shall prosper in the thing for which I sent it." Send forth the Word of God and force your circumstances to produce what you desire. Consider Ps. 107:20, "He sent His Word and healed them, and delivered them from all their destruction." 2 Peter 1:3 says, "His divine power has given us all things that pertain to life and godliness." God's divine power is His Word and He gives it to you to exercise dominion on the earth. Words spoken in faith put pressure on your circumstances. If you take dominion and believe what you're saying, it will come to pass. It has to because this is the law of seedtime and harvest (Gen. 8:22). Jesus said in Luke 17:6, "If you had faith as a mustard seed, you can say to this mulberry tree, 'Be pulled up by the roots and be planted in the sea,' and it would obey you." Did you catch that? Jesus said your circumstances will obey you when you take dominion over them.

You can have what you say if you believe and doubt not in your heart (Mark 11:23). When a circumstance tries to put pressure on you, turn around and speak the Word of God over it. Rom. 10:8 says, "The Word is near you, even in your mouth and your heart." Every time you speak the Word with authority you are taking dominion over your situation. You can sleep peacefully at night knowing the Word will produce what you sent it out to do. You were created to have lordship over all God's creation. You are responsible to rule and govern your domain, to be fruitful in everything you set your hand to do, bringing glory to God. When you take dominion you cultivate the earth with God's goodness, bringing order out of chaos. You are to execute your God-given authority to extend the blessings of God into all the world. To help you fulfill the dominion mandate and maximize your potential, God has placed within you a powerful anointing, which is God on flesh doing only what God can do (1 John 2:27).

With this anointing you are in possession of all that is necessary to take dominion over the earth and subdue it. Jesus was anointed and look at all the powerful works He did. The anointing is not a bunch of goosebumps you feel from time to time. No, it is the power of God at work in you. It helps you do what needs to be done in this sinful world. The anointing that dwells within cannot be activated and flow out of you until you first yield to it and respond to the pressures of life in a proper way. The anointing that abides in you will spring up only when you take dominion. All of a sudden God's power is working in you and through you in a higher and deeper level. The Holy Spirit is a gentleman and He won't force Himself and His anointing on anybody. He's not the one called to dominate; you are. Take dominion and yield to His mighty power. It's the anointing that removes the yoke of oppression from off your life (Is. 10:27). When the enemy comes in, like a flood the Lord will lift up a standard against him (Is. 59:19).

What is that standard? The anointing! When you take dominion, the Spirit does the work for you. Zech. 4:6 says, "Not by might nor by power, but by My Spirit says the Lord of hosts." According to the Bible, dominion is a God-given gift to mankind. It is the will of God for you to dominate in whatever you do and wherever you find yourself. All the King's men must manifest dominion in whatever they set their hand to do. People around you must be able to see God's glory in you as you live a life of dominion. To have dominion means to have victory over the evil one. Luke 10:19 says, "I have given you authority to trample on serpents and scorpions and to overcome all the power of the enemy." It means to excel in all things and to never settle for less. Deut. 28:13 says, "And the Lord will make you the head and not the tail; you shall be above only and not be beneath." The man who takes dominion cannot be defeated. He is victorious in every battle he fights.

Rise up for you are more than a conqueror and go from glory to glory. Hab. 2:4 says, "The just shall live by faith." A life of faith births the lifestyle of dominion. Faith enables you to be in charge and in control and to have dominion at all times. Faith is the vision of the invisible. It will cause you to be rooted and grounded and built up in the lifestyle of dominion and victory which in turn gives you access to a glorious destiny. You cannot live in dominion without acting in faith, without speaking the Word of God boldly. David confronted Goliath by boldly proclaiming God would deliver him into his hands. When you speak the Word boldly you'll have dominion and will be able to frame your world. You must then act on the Word of God believing it will do what God says it will do. By faith Jesus exercised dominion over the wind and waves and calmed them both. He spoke the Word, and it was so. Now is the time for you to do the same. Now is the time for you to take dominion.

# | 11 |

# "ENOUGH IS ENOUGH"

It is no secret how cunning and deceitful the devil is. He is truly a sly snake and has the ability to trick people in a subtle and covert way without revealing his true intentions. Snakes are often associated with deceit, hidden danger, and cunning behavior, making them a fitting metaphor for the devil's deceptive and evil nature. Unlike most other deadly creatures, snakes are small and can be hidden. They move quietly, strike unexpectedly, and often remain unseen until harm is done. Because of these traits, the serpent has long stood as a powerful metaphor for the devil's deceptive and evil nature. The enemy rarely approaches with obvious destruction. Instead, he comes subtly twisting truth, planting doubt, and disguising lies as harmless suggestions. Just as a snake blends into its surroundings, deception often hides in familiar places, appealing words, and half-truths. What appears small or insignificant can carry deadly venom if embraced.

The serpent's tactic has never changed. He questions God's Word, undermines trust, and entices with promises that lead to loss rather than life. His goal is not merely to frighten but to corrupt, not merely to attack but to seduce the mind and heart away from truth. Deception is his primary weapon, and distraction is his favorite strategy. The truth be told, many times you may not even know you have been bitten until the symptoms start. You're about to die a gruesome death and don't even know it. The devil always tries to mimic and counterfeit what is good. So deceptive is he that 2 Cor. 11:14 says, "Even Satan tries to make himself look like an angel of light." He deceives people by making the evil he wants them to do appear to be attractive, enjoyable, good, and moral. He doesn't tell you the pleasures of sin only last a moment. While sin may feel pleasurable for a moment, its enjoyment is temporary and will eventually lead to negative consequences, up to and including death (Rom. 6:23).

The good news is that all the King's men are not fooled by the deceitful ways of the devil. 2 Cor. 2:11 (TPT) says, "We would not be exploited by the adversary for we know his clever schemes." Ancient Chinese military general Sun Tzu once said, "If you know your enemy and know yourself, you need not fear the result of a hundred battles." Understanding yourself and your opponent is key to winning any confrontation. Knowing the enemy helps you take the offensive, knowing yourself helps you stand on the defensive. It comes as no surprise that the serpent is depicted as the tool used by Satan to tempt Eve in the Garden of Eden. It was there in the garden that Satan deceived Eve into thinking it was a good thing to have her eyes opened and to become like God, knowing good and evil (Gen. 3:5). Of course, we all know how that turned out. But what about Adam? What was he tempted to do? The answer is the devil tempted him with something that has destroyed men ever since.

Like a cancer that slowly spreads throughout the entire body, Adam was tempted with the epidemic of passivity. While deception unfolded, Adam stood by and did nothing as his wife sold her soul to the devil. Evil advances most rapidly where godly men remain passive. That moment of passivity opened the door to sin, brokenness, and generational pain. Ever since, passivity has been one of Satan's most effective weapons because it requires no effort. The devil whispers in the ears of men and tells them it's best to not make waves. Just sit still and do nothing and whatever happens, happens. Nothing is more deplorable than that. Edmund Burke said, "The only thing necessary for the triumph of evil is for good men to do nothing. All tyranny needs to gain a foothold is for good people to remain silent." Imagine that. Sin came into the world while Adam watched and did nothing. The devil knew then that to wreak havoc on the world all he has to do is get good men to do nothing.

So far, for the most part, this strategy has been working. All you have to do is look around and see the condition the world is currently in. It's bad and getting worse by the day. Passivity is the quiet surrender of responsibility, and it is destroying men, families, churches, and communities at an alarming rate. Men would rather record the evil being done on their phones than do something about it. The greatest damage in our generation is not always done by open rebellion, but by silent withdrawal. Many of the assaults of the enemy are spiritual and much more difficult to see the damage caused by their lack of action. Passivity seems harmless and this is the great deception. Men who are passive don't see what's at stake with their inactivity. Adam never imagined the long-term consequences of his passivity, but he should have. You need to know your enemy. He is a thief who comes only to steal and kill and destroy (John 10:10). Satan is aggressive, subtle, and smart. And he is not passive!

You must actively resist him! 1 Peter 5:8 says, "Be soberminded; be watchful. Your adversary the devil prowls around like a roaring lion, seeking someone to devour." Lions are brilliant and fierce hunters. Like these ferocious animals, the devil stalks his prey and has devoured many weak men. He wins every time when those he attacks do nothing. Vs. 9 (TPT) says, "Take a decisive stand against him and resist his every attack with strong, vigorous faith." In other words, pick up your sword and stop being passive! Peter makes it clear that you can defend yourself against the devil if you choose to. His power is real but very limited. He only wins when you fail to be active in resisting him. Men fail because it is so much easier to be passive, to sit back and do nothing. But all the King's men are different. They don't do what is easy, they do what is right. They know it is their God-given duty to reject passivity and accept responsibility. It is their calling to take a stand against the evil one and protect themselves and those they love.

They are not like Adam who knew what the right thing to do was but failed to do it. Instead of walking in fleshly passivity, they accept the call to walk in kingdom authority. In Matt. 28:18-20 Jesus leaves you with authority and in Acts 1:8 He gives you power. With His authority and power, you have everything you need to defeat the enemy every time. Kingdom authority is the right and responsibility of every man to act and rule under the King, on behalf of the King, and for the King. You do not have the right to be passive. It is time to stop seeing yourself as a worm crawling in the dust. The problem is most men see themselves as the devil sees them instead of how God sees them. In Luke 10:9 Jesus sent seventy disciples out two by two and gave them the authority to heal the sick and to bring forth the manifestation of the power of God on the earth. They were able to defeat the enemy because they were given the authority to do so. 2 Tim. 1:7 says, "For God has not given us a spirit of fear, but of power and love and of a sound mind."

God has given you the spirit of power. When you have knowledge of the power that has been delegated to you, you'll then have the faith to operate in it. Watch what happens in Luke 10:17, "Then the seventy returned with joy, saying, 'Lord, even the demons are subject to us in Your name.'" To their delight, the demons were brought under their control, made subordinate to them in Jesus' Name. Charles Spurgeon said, "Not one of the lambs had been eaten by the wolves." Matt. 8:5-13 tells how a Roman centurion told Jesus about his paralyzed servant. Jesus agreed to go heal the man, but the centurion told Him to use His authority instead. He said to Jesus, "I am not worthy that You should come under my roof. But only speak a word, and my servant will be healed" (vs. 8). Those in the military understand authority. He said, "For I am a man under authority, having soldiers under me. I say to this one, 'Go,' and he goes; and to another, 'Come,' and he comes; and to my servant, 'Do this,' and he does it" (vs. 9).

Notice that whatever the centurion commanded his soldiers and servants to do, they immediately obeyed without a moment of hesitation. This is the power of authority. If he could give orders that were promptly obeyed, certainly Jesus, the possessor of greater authority, could do the same and much, much more. Because this man understood authority, Jesus marveled at his words. He said to those in the crowd, "I have not found so great faith, not even in Israel!" (vs. 10). "Then Jesus said to the centurion, 'Go your way; and as you have believed, so let it be done for you.' And his servant was healed the same hour" (vs. 13). Miracles do not happen by accident, and they are not reserved for a special few. They flow naturally when a believer understands and operates in the authority that God has already given. Many men pray for power when they have been called to walk in authority. Yield yourself to God and His power and authority will flow through you.

Authority unused is authority wasted. Miracles do not respond to knowledge alone - they respond to exercised authority. Jesus never struggled to get results because He never questioned His authority. He spoke to sickness, commanded storms, rebuked demons, and declared freedom because He knew who He was, where He stood, and what Heaven backed. Authority is not about volume, emotion, or effort. Authority is about position. When you understand your position in Christ, your words carry weight in the spirit realm. When believers speak with spiritual authority, circumstances must respond. Not because of who they are in themselves, but because of who stands behind them. Jesus said in Luke 10:19, "Behold, I give you authority to trample on serpents and scorpions, and over all the power of the enemy, and nothing shall by any means hurt you." You can rejoice exceedingly knowing the devil has no power over you. In fact, just the opposite is true. It is you who has supernatural power and authority over him and all his minions.

Yes, it is you who has power and might over the kingdom of darkness. Ps. 91:13 says, "You will tread upon the lion and cobra, the young lion and serpent you shall trample underfoot." When fear is stripped away, readiness takes its place. A heart anchored in God does not shrink back when the call comes - it rises. With nothing to fear, you are forever prepared to engage in any battle God calls you into. Why? Because your confidence is not in yourself, but in the One who sends you. When you know who you are in God, hesitation fades and obedience becomes decisive. You don't argue with the assignment; you step into it. You don't question your authority; you walk in it. The absence of fear doesn't mean the absence of danger - it means the presence of trust. You trust that God goes before you, stands beside you, and guards your rear. God does not call the timid to fight with uncertainty. He calls the willing to stand with courage. When He says, "Go," you go. When He says, "Fight," you fight.

You understand that the battle is not yours to win by force, but His to accomplish through obedience. Being ready for war doesn't mean craving conflict; it means refusing retreat. It means knowing that peace with God produces boldness before opposition. You don't fight because you are angry - you fight because you are assigned. You don't move out of fear of the enemy - you move out of reverence for God. With nothing to fear, you are always ready to advance, ready to confront, ready to obey. You rise, you engage, and you walk forward in the authority He has placed upon your life. Jesus said in Luke 10:18, "I saw Satan fall like lightning from heaven." Satan loses his power when you begin to operate in kingdom authority. You can cast him down forevermore. 1 John 3:8 says Jesus came to destroy the works of the devil and so are you to do the same thing. How? By no longer being passive and by operating in kingdom authority.

You are called to take a stand against the schemes of the devil (Eph. 6:10,11), to stand firm against him (1 Peter 5:8,9), and to resist him at all times (James 4:7). This was demonstrated in Acts 16:18 when Paul cast an evil spirit out of a slave girl. He said, "I command you in the name of Jesus to come out of her." And he came out that very hour. The demon left the girl in obedience to Paul's command because he operated in kingdom authority. The words had scarcely left his lips when she was released from her life of torment. Likewise, all the King's men are called to step in and intervene when they see someone being spiritually assaulted by the enemy. It is their responsibility to tell the devil, "Enough is enough!" Like Jesus being tempted in the wilderness, you are not to sit passively by and do nothing. No, you stand against the devil by the power of the Spirit and the truth of God's Word. The enemy thrives where there is passivity, but he retreats when a man of God rises in authority.

The devil is a trespasser, not an owner. He has no legal right to your life, your family, your peace, or your future unless you allow him space. Jesus has already won the victory, but you must enforce it. Victory is provided by Christ, yet resistance is practiced by the believer. Being one of the King's men is a wonderful calling so make sure you're walking in your God-given authority as the leader God called you to be in every area God has assigned to you. What should Adam have done when Satan approached his wife and began to lie to her? He should have taken a stand against the enemy on her behalf. He should have protected her. You cannot be passive and stand aside when you see injustice being done, when you see someone under attack. God put a sword in your hand not to lay it down but to use it. Can you imagine the world we'd be in today if Adam would have pointed his finger at that serpent and said, "I command you to leave this garden and never come back!"?

Jesus said in Matt. 16:19, "And I will give you the keys of the kingdom of heaven, and whatever you bind on earth will be bound in heaven, and whatever you loose on earth, will be loosed in heaven." That's kingdom authority! Keys represent authority to declare what is bound and loosed in heaven. When the King of kings gives authority to His people, they carry it wherever they go. A trusted steward kept the keys of his master's possessions and dispensed them accordingly. With kingdom authority you can bind the devil and loose the blessings of God on the earth. Learn to view life and the situations you face with the understanding that the kingdom of God is within you and that He had placed authority, power, and dominion in you. Kingdom authority is available to every believer. God has authorized you to act on His behalf and to have access to His divine power, overcoming obstacles in every area of life. God desires to work in you and through you, to see you be in purposeful alignment with His will.

God showed us how kingdom authority works in the story of creation back in the book of Genesis. Gen. 1:2,3 says, "Darkness was on the face of the deep. And the Spirit of God was hovering over the face of the waters. Then God said, 'Let there be light' and there was light." That was kingdom authority at work. Darkness was all around until God spoke with authority. Notice the Spirit of God was already there but nothing happened until words were spoken with authority. Jesus said in John 6:63, "The words I speak to you are spirit and they are life." Heb. 4:12 says, "For the word of God is living and powerful, and sharper than any two-edged sword." There is authority in the spoken Word of God. God saw the darkness but spoke what He desired. The Spirit who was there had nothing to work with until God spoke words of authority. The story of creation teaches us there is power and authority in the spoken word. To not understand that is to give the enemy free reign to sow havoc in your life.

God said what He wanted and multiple times it says, "And it was so" (vs. 7,9,11,15,24,30). This tells us that words spoken with authority are fulfilled without fail. Don't miss the importance of this small phrase. It's saying that what God wanted wasn't so until He said it. Whatever He said happened the way He designed it. The phrase "and it was so" is repeated each time God speaks and something is created. It indicates that God's intentions are carried out and that the power of kingdom authority is not limited. One of the first things we learn in the Bible is the concept of kingdom authority. God used it to create the heavens and the earth and we are to us it today. People pray, "As it was in the beginning, is now, and ever shall be, world without end. Amen." In other words, as kingdom authority was in the beginning, so it forever shall be on the earth. 2 Cor. 4:13 says, "I believed and therefore I spoke." As long as what you say lines up with the Word of God, whatever you declare with kingdom authority will come to pass.

Use your authority to speak forth what God has promised. Declare by the authority given to you that what the Bible says you can have is yours and it will be so for you. Every problem in the world can be overcome with kingdom authority. As God framed the universe with words of authority, so can you frame your world with what you say and do. Do you want to live a victorious life? Then go back to the story of creation and learn about kingdom authority. Eph. 5:1 (MSG) says, "Watch what God does, and then you do it." Do you want to be made whole in every area of your life? Then frame your world and speak to your bank account and your job. Speak to your high blood pressure, diabetes, and heart disease. Speak words of life into your marriage and your troubled and depressed mind. Let the weak say "I am strong" (Joel 3:10) and let the poor say, "I am rich." Prov. 18:21 says, "Death and life are in the power of the tongue and those who love it will eat its fruit." The words you speak today frame the world you'll live in tomorrow.

God works with your words and Jesus is even called the High Priest of your confession (Heb. 3:1). Your words are molding and shaping what's going to happen in your life. God framed the worlds with His words, and you frame your world with yours. You frame prosperity and health and soundness of mind by what comes out of your mouth. Speaking with kingdom authority is how God ordained you to live. Confess daily that with long life God will satisfy you and show you His salvation (Ps. 91:16). Once you speak forth what you want, then with faith look for the fulfillment of God's promised Word. Heb. 11:10 says Abraham looked forward to the city whose builder and maker is God. Ask and you shall receive. Seek and you will find. With kingdom authority you have the full assurance that what you're believing for will come to pass. So start looking for it. Expectation causes faith to rise up inside of you and when it does you look for the blessing and keep looking. Soon it will be there for you to enjoy. And it was so.

# | 12 |

# "BOLD AS A LION"

All real men of God are strong warriors. If they weren't, they wouldn't be in the army of the Lord. Daily they fearlessly fight for the glory and honor of their Lord and Savior. Why are they so strong? Because God makes them strong. 2 Tim. 1:7 says to all men, "For God has not given us a spirit of fear, but of power and of love and of a sound mind." The Amplified Bible says, "For God did not give us a spirit of timidity or cowardice or fear, but He has given us a spirit of power and of love and of sound judgment and personal discipline." The virtue of power, added to the virtues of love and a sound mind, will produce a supernatural boldness on the inside of you. You'll be empowered to take action regardless of risks. What is boldness? It's the courage to act or speak fearlessly despite real or imagined dangers. David said in Ps. 27:1, "The Lord is the strength of my life, of whom shall I be afraid?"

David declared where his strength came from because he knew we are only as strong as the source of our strength. Eph. 6:10 says we are to "be strong in the Lord and in the power of His might." You become bold when you know inside of you is the omnipotent power of God that overcomes resistance and effects a change. No giant can withstand you when you are empowered by God. David was filled with boldness when he said to Goliath, "You come to me with a sword, with a spear, and with a javelin. But I come to you in the name of the Lord of hosts" (1 Sam. 17:45). He understood his source of strength and this is what made him bold. He said, "This day the Lord will deliver you into my hand, and I will strike you and take your head from you" (vs. 46). With no fear he said, "Then all this assembly shall know that the Lord does not save with sword and spear; for the battle is the Lord's, and He will give you into our hands" (vs. 47).

"For God has said, 'I will never leave you nor forsake you.' So we may boldly say, 'The Lord is my helper so I will have no fear. What can mere people do to me?'" (Heb. 13:5,6). This is the attitude and confession of all the King's men. They're forever bold and never let the spirit of darkness intimidate them and cause them to run and hide in a hole somewhere. Christianity is not a powerless faith. 1 Cor. 2:5 says, "That your faith should not be in the wisdom of men but in the power of God." Always are we to trust in His almighty power. This is real power and it changes people's lives. It will make you bold and strong. Prov. 28:1 says, "The wicked flee when no one pursues, but the righteous are bold as a lion." Prov. 30:30 says, "A lion is the strongest among beasts and turns not away from anything." We are designed by God to be bold and to never back down from any challenge.

Boldness is like a light in the darkness and was one of the first characteristics the Holy Spirit imparted when He came to indwell believers after Jesus ascended into heaven. The disciples faced persecution from the authorities so they prayed, "Lord, look on their threats, and grant to Your servants that with all boldness they may speak Your word" (Acts 4:29). God gives us boldness when our objective is to obey and glorify Him with it. Their prayers were answered "and they were all filled with the Holy Spirit and they spoke the Word of God with boldness" (vs. 31). Godly boldness is motivated by a deep passion for Christ. When Paul was in prison he wrote to the churches asking for prayer that he be bold in continuing to preach the gospel (Eph. 6:19). For Paul, to speak boldly would probably mean more persecution for him but he didn't care. Why? Because he was convinced that the message he preached could change the world.

Heb. 4:16 says, "Let us therefore come fearlessly and confidently and boldly to the throne of grace, that we may obtain mercy and find grace to help in time of need." We can go boldly before God with humble confidence knowing He welcomes us with opened arms. He invites all His people to come and sit at His feet in His holy presence. It's in the presence of God when you boldly say, "No weapon formed against me shall prosper" (Is. 54:17). You need to believe this because bold prayers are in reality a declaration of war. Like the disciples in the book of Acts, you also need to pray and ask God to make you bold as a lion, to give you unshakeable spiritual conviction and the courage to obey Him no matter the cost. The disciples prayed for boldness and that "signs and wonders may be done through the name of Your holy Servant Jesus" (Acts 4:30). Immediately the place where they were assembled was shaken (vs. 31).

God answered their prayer and all the religious leaders were amazed at how bold they were. Are people amazed at your boldness? Are they aware that you are a servant of the Most High God? Be bold and walk in such a way that everybody will know that you are a committed disciple of Jesus Christ. Your very presence alone represents the goodness and grace of God. To those who are meek and timid and more quiet than others understand that, from a biblical sense, boldness is   not a personality trait, it's the result of the Holy Spirit working in your life. When the Holy Spirit comes upon you, you can be naturally quiet and laid back and suddenly be filled with spiritual courage and speak the Word of God boldly and without hesitation. Just know that if you pray for boldness, you will be given by God opportunities to be bold in ways you have never seen before. He'll prompt you to speak the Word of God boldly all for His glory.

Pray for boldness with faith believing that God will show up and do what only He can do. In the midst of great persecution Peter and John kept on preaching Jesus and the gospel message. Because of their boldness miracles happened and people got saved. The religious leaders did not like this so they "laid their hands on the apostles and put them in the public jail" (Acts 5:18). If you have the courage to pray, "God, make me bold as a lion," know that this will trigger spiritual opposition. War has been declared and persecution may become a thorn in your flesh like it was with Paul. But that's okay. "If God be for us, who can be against us?" (Rom. 8:31). With God on your side, all fear of successful opposition is removed and this makes you more bold. If God is for us, it makes no difference who is against us. God said to Abraham, "Do not fear, Abram, I am a shield to you; Your reward will be very great" (Gen. 15:1).

Yes, persecution and opposition will come. But remember what God told Jeremiah, "They will fight against you, but they will not overcome you, for I am with you to deliver you" (Jer. 1:19). Charles Spurgeon said of those who would come against you, "There are many, but they are nothing, nor all put together anything at all, as compared to Him who is on our side." The righteous are bold as a lion. Their war cry is, "God is for us!" Though all the world is against you, you can shake all the world the same way Samson shook the lion (Judges 14:6). We all need the strength and boldness of Martin Luther who said, "I am rough, boisterous, stormy, and altogether warlike, fighting against innumerable monsters and devils. I am born for the removing of stumps and stones, cutting away thistles and thorns, and clearing the wild forests." Here was a bold man on a mission to bring glory to his God.

All the King's men are trained and prepared for spiritual warfare. They know that if they're not ready to face opposition for their obedience to God, they're not ready to be used by God. They press forward against the forces of darkness knowing their boldness will release the miracles of God. With bold faith you'll see the hand of God move in a powerful way. Peter and John were in jail for preaching the gospel when suddenly "at night an angel of the Lord opened the prison doors and brought them out" (Acts 5:19). That is a miracle. No where does it say the disciples were surprised by this miracle. The truth is, when you're bold as a lion and walking in obedience to God, you shouldn't be surprised when the supernatural happens. When you're bold you'll set in motion the faithfulness and miraculous power of God. This will happen but first you must believe it will happen because boldness always requires faith.

The angel said to them, "Go to the temple and give the people this message of life" (vs. 20). In other words, go do the same thing that got them arrested in the first place. How did they respond knowing to obey might get them killed? Vs. 21 says, "So at daybreak the apostles entered the temple as they were told and immediately began teaching." It took faith to do this. When you pray for boldness, be prepared for the Spirit to prompt you to do something that requires faith on your part. Be ready for it will indeed happen. And when you obey what the Spirit tells you to do in faith, rest assured, a miracle is on its way. Great things can and will happen through a single act of bold obedience. Know with confidence that behind the scenes God is always working. Don't fret or worry when you face opposition for boldly doing what God tells you to do. Worry when you don't.

What makes all the King's men different from other men is they want to be bold. They want their light to shine in a dark world. They want to make this world a better place. So strong is their love for God and people they don't care if they face opposition. The deep desire of their heart is for all people to know the freedom and grace that is theirs through Christ. Forever bold are the warriors of Christ. Empowered by the Spirit they go out into the world around them to show people the glory and the love and the goodness of the living God. Time is quickly passing by and now is the time to be bold as a lion. It's time to get out of your comfort zone and do what God is calling you to do. Remember, evil prevails when good men do nothing. Boldness is a gift of the Spirit so use it often. The truth be told, it matters how you say things. People will listen when you boldly speak in a clear and concise manner.

Eagerly seek to be more bold and more fearless and to have the force of character to speak up for what's right, to have the same strength and power the disciples had in the days of the early church. Live in such a way that your enthusiasm for God swells up on the inside of you, so much so that you can't keep it to yourself, but you boldly speak it out to others. Use your boldness as a magnet to draw people into the kingdom of God. Let God use you and there will certainly be an irresistible attraction that will bring people to their knees. It is boldness that brings people to Christ. Boldly tell others what Christ has done for you. Speak with true conviction in the power of the Spirit and people will listen to you. The world is not looking for eloquent speakers but those who speak from the heart. Speak with feeling and the Holy Spirit will take your boldness and melt the hearts of the people.

Good things happen when you're bold as a lion. Like a lion, the righteous have a conscience that is clear and pure. They go forward knowing they are guided and protected by God

Almighty. Lions are a symbol of boldness, courage, strength, and power. They walk through the jungle unafraid of anything. Other animals flee when he approaches and cowers at his mighty roar. Lions inspire fear and respect through being impressively large, powerful, intimidating, and very awesome. The lion is fearless and dominate wherever he goes, just as you are to be. Oh, how majestic and commanding a lion is. He is powerful and sovereign among animals. All the King's men are to be like them for there is nothing like the fierceness of a lion. The man who is bold as a lion does not worry. He is confident that he is protected by the Lord and walks with Him daily. All he does is guaranteed, blessed, and certain to triumph in the end.

Men who are bold behave in a controlled manner and are filled with good judgment and discernment. They live with confidence because they fear God and do their best to please Him. They are bold and secure and walk about with courage and confidence. Jesus said in John 16:33, "In the world you will have tribulation but be of good cheer, I have overcome the world." We need courage and boldness to do the Lord's work here in the last days because perilous times are upon us. The same boldness and bravery the first century disciples had is now required of us. Now is not the time to shrink back but boldly go forward and complete the task God has set before us. We can't let anything stop us from completing the calling God has placed on our lives. Consider what the Bible says about Paul in Acts 28:31, "He proclaimed the kingdom of God and taught about the Lord Jesus Christ will all boldness and without hindrance."

Lions are afraid of nothing so don't overestimate your opponent and certainly don't underestimate yourself. Your Savior is the Lion of Judah (Rev. 5:5) and you are in Him and He is in you. Spending time in His Word will make you bold because you will see yourself as God sees you. You are the righteousness of God in Christ Jesus (2 Cor. 5:21) and have no excuse to be timid in this life. God is looking for strong men to go into the enemy's camp and take back what belongs to Him. It takes boldness and courage to do that. Rise up and go in the direction God calls you to go. Know that when you start on this journey there is no turning back. Heb. 10:38 says, "Now the just shall live by faith; But if anyone draws back, My soul has no pleasure in him." This is the Lord speaking. Clearly He takes no pleasure when you shrink back from what He's called you to do. It is the objective of the enemy to stop you from finishing what you started.

Thankfully we read in Heb. 10:39 (TPT), "But we are certainly not those who are held back by fear and perish; we are among those who have faith and experience true life." Men who are bold as a lion never draw back because they know God is on their side. They know they are surrounded by an army of angelic hosts in the unseen heavenly realm. They know it's time to show the devil who's boss. Matt. 11:12 says, "From the days of John the Baptist until now the kingdom of heaven suffers violence, and the violent take it by force." Holy violence is spiritual zeal that causes a man with boldness to press forward relentlessly until he recovers everything the enemy has stolen from the children of God. Charles Spurgeon said, "When God makes a man violent after salvation, that man cannot perish.

The gates of heaven may sooner be unhinged than that man be robbed of the prize for which he has fought."

Sad to say, boldness is lacking in the average Christian man. Most of them do not act like lions. They seem almost scared to let people know they are Christians. You need to realize that boldness must be built on a firm foundation. Consider what Paul said in 1 Thess. 2:2, "We were bold in our God to speak to you the gospel of God in much conflict." His close relationship with God was the foundation his boldness was built on. Speaking of Jesus, he said in Eph. 3:12, "In Whom we have boldness." In other words, you received boldness the day you got saved. That settles the matter. You do not have to pray for boldness, work for it, or hope for it. You already have it. The question is, what are you doing with it? Since God has given you boldness, don't let it lay dormant but rise up and use it fully and use it often. Let it be manifested as you do the things God has called you to do.

After Paul got saved he "preached boldly at Damascus in the name of Jesus" (Acts 9:27). He spoke freely, openly, fearlessly, and boldly. All the King's men are called to do the same. Paul spoke about Jesus without any sense of fear or constraint because he was bold as a lion. He knew it was necessary to manifest his boldness when taking a stand for his Lord and Savior. People today are hurting and desperate for help. They're looking for someone to come along to take them by the hand and place them on the path that leads to an abundant life. There are many types of people on the earth but only one kind who will make this world a better place. Those who make a positive difference are the righteous who are bold as a lion. God is calling you to be that person. You're to love boldly, live boldly, speak boldly. Remember, you already have boldness. Now rise up and use it for the glory of God.

# | 13 |

# "THE PERFECT WARRIOR"

Picture in your mind the perfect warrior, a man born and bred to fight. Demanded of him would be an extreme loyalty to his master and a willingness to die for the cause for which he fought. A restless, flame-like emotion derived from an intense devotion to his beliefs will compel him to display vigorous and untiring activity in its support. He would have to be a leader of men, a skilled marksman, fervent in spirit, and most important of all, he would have to possess and maintain an excessive zeal for whatever undertaking he was engaged in. Such a man was Jehu, the son of Nimshi. He drove his chariot with vigor and speed, he was an expert with the arrow and bow, and he was a naturally born leader who commanded the respect of his loyal followers. One day Jehu was gathered together with the captions of the Israelite army when a messenger sent from the prophet Elisha came to him at Ramoth-Gilead.

This messenger, who was one of the sons of the prophets, poured oil on his head and said, "Thus says the Lord God of

Israel, 'I have anointed you king over the people of the Lord, over Israel! You shall strike down the house of Ahab, your master, that I may avenge the blood of My servants the prophets, and the blood of all the servants of the Lord at the hand of Jezebel. For the whole house of Ahab shall perish'" (2 Kings 9:6-8). Here was a man anointed by God who was given the power to do what only God could do. Watch what happens next. A fierce and passionate fervor rose up in the heart of Jehu as he immediately set out to obey the orders just given him. Nothing would stand in his way. His first destination was Jezreel, the home of the evil Jezebel and her equally wicked son Joram, the ailing king whom Jehu has replaced.

After piercing his wicked predecessor in the heart with a perfectly aimed arrow, Jehu gave the order to the servants of Jezebel to throw their treacherous and sinful queen down from a balcony on which she sat. When they did, Jehu drove his chariot over her body and shortly thereafter a prophecy spoken by Elijah was fulfilled when wild dogs tore her body to pieces. After this, Jehu had every member of Ahab's family put to death along with all his close acquaintances and priests. More killings followed as Jehu faithfully continued to fulfill the assignment bestowed upon him. One day a messenger named Jehonadab met the anointed king on the roadway and Jehu invited him to climb up into his chariot so they could ride together. Jehu then made a unique invitation to his new passenger, "Come with me and see my zeal for the Lord" (2 Kings10:16). He then made one of the greatest turnarounds ever made by a king anointed by God. Or so it seemed.

After killing all that remained to Ahab in Samaria, Jehu announced that God was no longer his Lord and that he had decided to follow and worship Baal, the god of Ahab and all his followers. He boldly declared, "Ahab served Baal a little but Jehu will serve him much" (vs. 18). He then arranged for a great feast and sent for all the worshippers of Baal to come and make a great sacrifice to their god. People came from all over the kingdom and the temple was filled from one end to the other. Jehu then ordered his men to "search and see that no servants of the Lord are here, but only the worshippers of Baal" (vs. 23). When this was completed, Jehu commanded his soldiers to surround the temple and to kill every Baal priest in the place. Afterward they went out and destroyed every idol throughout the land. This great slaughter was carried out because Jehu had a "zeal for the Lord." His aggressive actions may appear to be gruesome but Jehu carried out precisely the orders given to him by the Lord.

Jehu was a warrior to the utmost and zeal is a weapon used in warfare. It creates in you a deep desire and willingness to be used by God to help destroy the works of the enemy. Eccl. 9:10 says, "Whatever your hand finds to do, do it with might." Also, Col. 3:23 tells us, "Whatever you do, work at it with all your heart as working for the Lord, not for men." Zeal births in you an intense enthusiasm and eagerness to do what is good and it gives you the confidence to complete whatever you begin. The story of Jehu reveals that zeal was an everyday part of his life. He personified the words of Deut. 30:20, "That you may love the Lord your God, that you may obey His voice, and that you may cling to Him." This verse describes perfectly the three main attributes of having a "zeal for the Lord." First and foremost, you shall love the Lord your God with all your heart, with all your soul, and with all your mind" (Matt. 22:37).

Next, you will obey His voice with no reservation or doubt. 1 Sam. 15:22 says, "Has the Lord as great delight in burnt offerings and sacrifices as in obeying the voice of the Lord? Behold, to obey is better than sacrifice." Finally, we are to cling to Him. Jesus tells us in John 15:4 to "Abide in Me, and I in you." James mirrors this sentiment when he writes, "Draw near to God and He will draw near to you" (James 4:8). All the King's men are all called to be warriors for the Lord. Jesus said, "Do not think that I came to bring peace on earth. I did not come to bring peace but a sword" (Matt. 10:34). Zeal is an expression of our faith in Jesus as our military commander and since faith is an action so then must zeal lead us to action. After all, that's what being a warrior is all about. Always be ready and willing to be used by God to destroy the works of the enemy. Follow in the footsteps of Jehu and be aggressive and determined as you set out to fulfill your calling from the Lord.

Jesus said He came to bring not peace but a sword. He demonstrated this twice when He overturned tables and drove the money-changers out of the temple. Charles Spurgeon said, "He wars against war, and contends against contention. In the act of producing the peace of heaven, He arouses the rage of hell." That's the God we serve. Yes, Jesus is the great peacemaker but before peace He brings war. Something supernatural came over Him when He saw His Father's house being violated by those who bought and sold there. That something was zeal.

John 2:17 says that as the disciples tried to process this moment they remembered what David said in Ps. 69:9, "Zeal for Your house has consumed me." Jehu was consumed by zeal and so was Jesus. The Greek word "zelos" means 'to be hot; to boil, to burn, to glow.' It describes fervor in advancing a cause or in rendering service.

Having a zeal for the Lord means you'll have a single-minded allegiance to Him at all times. With enthusiastic devotion and an undivided heart you'll pursue His purpose for your life. So strong is your eagerness to please your Master that you'll be consumed with what He wants you to do. The Greek word "katesthio" means 'to eat up; swallow; devour.' Jesus was consumed with a love for His Father's house. It ate Him up when He saw it being used as a place to do business instead of using it as a house of prayer. Being zealous will fill you with great energy, effort, and enthusiasm. Charles Spurgeon said, "His burning passion, like the flame of a candle, fed on His strength and consumed it." All the King's men must follow in the footsteps of Jesus and be consumed with zeal. Titus 2:14 says Jesus came to "purify for Himself His own special people, zealous for good works."

To be one of the King's men you must forever be serving the Lord with a holy fervor. There is a certain intensity in the life of a man and you must have a boiling spirit and keep yourself fueled and aflame. All the true men of God have a passion that burns like fire. Christian martyr Jim Elliot expressed his zeal when he said, "Saturate me with the oil of the Spirit that I may be a flame." Methodist minister Samuel Chadwick said, "Men ablaze war invincible. Hell trembles when men kindle." Let's not forget that in Acts 2:3 the Holy Spirit came like tongues of fire on the disciples. When you're zealous, you're burning on the inside. You'll burn with passion and intensity. Zeal has strong feelings. When zeal take over it affects your spirit and consumes your emotions. Jesus walked into the temple with burning emotions. He was angry. He was jealous. He was grieved. He was boiling with passion and intensity. He was consumed with zeal.

Zeal is more than just a feeling. It is an overwhelming enthusiasm that leads to action. Zeal serves. Zeal moves. Zeal always presses forward. Zeal is unable to stand still. Rom. 12:11 (TPT) says, "Be enthusiastic to serve the Lord, keeping your passion toward Him boiling hot. Radiate with the glow of the Holy Spirit and let Him fill you with excitement as you serve Him." The Philips Bible says, "Let us not allow slackness to spoil our work, and let us keep the fires of our spirit burning as we do our work for the Lord." The NIV says "never be lacking in zeal" and this is a rebuke to passivity, laziness, lethargy, apathy, and boredom. This means you must be earnest, zealous, on fire, and enthusiastic in serving the Lord. We exist to spread a passion for the supremacy of God in all things so have a burning zeal to do the will of God. With fervor and enthusiasm you must find ways to pour your life into the things of God.

Theologian William MacDonald said, "No disciple can be excused if he does not have zeal. If his heart is not aflame with a red-hot passion for the Savior, he stands condemned." He also said, "A zealous man in religion is a man of one thing. He only sees one thing, he cares for one thing, he is swallowed up in one thing, and that one thing is to please God." All the King's men are disciplined by divine grace and actively seek to know God and make Him known. They are white-hot and on fire for everything that is right and true. The source of all Christian zeal is an understanding of the glory. holiness, and all-out magnificence of God. Those who have a small vision of God will have no zeal. Having a head full of knowledge of God, a heart full of passion, and a life full of action is what godly zeal is all about. It's marked by active interest and enthusiasm.

John Wesley once wrote, "Get on fire for God and men will come and see you burn." Zeal is truly a mark of honor and it is to burn inside of you until you warm and enlighten others. Anglican bishop J. C. Ryle said zeal impels men "to deny themselves and make any sacrifice, to go through any trouble, to suffer, to work, and even to die, if only he can please God and honor Christ." Take heed to what Paul said in Titus 3:14, "And let our people also learn to maintain good works, to meet urgent needs, that they may not be unfruitful." The TPT says, "Encourage the believers to be passionately devoted to beautiful works of righteousness by meeting the urgent needs of others and not be unfruitful." We should be living so that people will know their worth in Christ. Oswald Chambers said, "Do good until it is an unconscious habit of life and you do not know you are doing it."

Rev. 1:12-16 is a vision of Jesus Christ in blazing splendor. The call of God on all the King's men is to be set ablaze with boiling zeal just as He is ablaze with glory. We are here to make

His glory known to all the nations and this is why zeal is not something we just passively hope for, it is something we must aggressively pursue. Zeal is not just another character trait we cultivate, it is the primary mark of the men of God. God demands it and we should not settle for anything less than it. God has always wanted men whose hearts are filled with passion and affection for Him. This is what it means to "love the Lord your God with all your heart, soul, and strength" (Deut. 6:5). To be zealous is a direct command from God. Stop settling for a life that has no passion in it. A man who is not fervent in spirit will become lukewarm through compromise.

Compromise is like erosion, it happens slowly and before you know it you're in a state of lukewarmness and you're only going through the motions. Those who have lost their fervency and passion for God become empty, slack, shallow, sluggish, and useless. Those who are not on fire on the inside will not do very much on the outside. Passivity and its do-nothing attitude is unacceptable to God and slothfulness should never be tolerated. The wet blanket of apathy, sloth, and laziness will put out your fire for God. Don't drag your feet spiritually but be full of zeal, forever glowing in your spirit. The word "fervor" suggests heat and passion and only the fervency of the Spirit can overcome laziness and slothfulness. The heat of one's fervency will drive you forward and cause you to wake up each morning ready and willing to be used by God to serve Him and bless others.

Paul said in 1 Cor. 15:58, "Therefore, my beloved brethren, be steadfast, immovable, always abounding in the work of the

Lord, knowing that your labor is not in vain in the Lord." God has assigned us much to accomplish and He will hold us accountable for the faithful performance of it. All the King's men have enough to do to occupy all his time until the Lord returns. He whose life is spent in ease and does nothing should doubt altogether his faith in God and whether or not he is truly saved. Jesus said, "He who believes in Me, the works that I do he will do also" (John 14:12). Being fervent in spirit is the capacity and ability of every man to be consumed and eaten up by the things of God. The call on your life is to do the will of God from the heart. Serving God is fun and the Christian attitude must be one of enthusiasm, a hot fervor which the Spirit promotes. Ps. 100:2 says, "Serve the Lord with gladness; Come before His presence with singing."

A joyful spirit is a fervent spirit in which the fire of your first love still burns. You will succeed if the fire of faith, hope, and love burns brightly from within. Jesus said John the Baptist was "the burning and shining lamp" (John 5:35) and in Matt. 5:16 He said, "Let your light so shine before men, that they may see your good works and glorify your Father in heaven." This is a great motivator to be fervent in spirit because the brighter and hotter your light shines, the more glory the Lord receives. Your sole desire is to serve Him with enthusiasm that comes from having a fervent heart. In the context of Christian service "fervent" means 'to be full of energy, to be on fire with zeal and enthusiasm.' It is a warning against settling into comfortable, shallow ruts in your spiritual life. The idea is that you are to be continually "hot" for the things of God. It is to be your habitual practice, your lifestyle before a critically watching world.

Zeal begins with an all-consuming vision of the glory of God and it moves from our head and then to our heart and finally to our hands. Zeal always leads to action. Your love and devotion has no ultimate value unless you are humbly and fervently serving the Lord. Work for Christ with feeling and live for Him with all your might. Intensity matters, zeal matters, wholeheartedness matters (see Jer. 29:13,14). Don't settle for anything less. Work for Christ passionately and be eager and earnest to accomplish what He has called you to do. Live your life in such a way that it shows openly your love and adoration for Him. Those who are great have a strong desire to worship and serve and are always looking for opportunities to do so. Col. 3:2 says, "Set your mind on things above, not on things on the earth." There are great things worth living for, such as the greatness of God and His glorious purposes in the world.

We exist to spread a passion for the supremacy of God in all things. Serving God is not for the weak and timid and this is why you must boil in your spirit and stir up zeal for God, and the cause of truth and life. Rom. 14:8 says, "For if we live, we live to the Lord; and if we die, we die to the Lord. Therefore, whether we live or die, we are the Lord's." All of life is a serving of the Lord and there is a work to be done. Work is spiritual. The Father works, the Son works, and you are to work also. This is why you must make godly zeal the primary pursuit of your life. Serving others is what gives meaning to life and brings complete satisfaction. Total fulfillment comes when God uses you to help another person's dream come true. This only happens when you love God more than you love yourself and when you desire what God wants more than what you want. Truly, it will be the most fulfilling life you could ever imagine.

# | 14 |

# "TEACH US TO PRAY"

M att. 21:12 tells the story of Jesus cleansing the temple of the moneychangers who sold there. He turned over tables, drove the people out, and caused massive chaos. Yes, Jesus is the sweet, tender Lamb of God who takes away the sins of the world. But He is also the Lion of the tribe of Judah and He displays righteous anger when appropriate. This is one of those times and He told the people why He did it. He said in vs. 13, "My house shall be called a house of prayer, but you have made it a den of thieves." Think about it. The same Jesus who played with children and conversed gently with the Samaritan woman was the same Jesus who made a whip and overturned tables. When Jesus entered the temple and overturned the tables of the moneychangers, He revealed a side of Himself that many struggle to understand. Yet this moment does not contradict His love, gentleness, or mercy - it reveals the depth of His holiness. His anger that day was properly motivated, rightly focused, and self-controlled.

Jesus was not angry because His ego was bruised. He was not reacting emotionally or losing control. He was not acting out of frustration or personal offense. Jesus' anger was born out of love for God and compassion for people. The temple - meant to be a place of prayer - had been turned into a marketplace of greed. Worship was being corrupted, and the poor were being exploited. His zeal flowed from a deep desire to honor His Father and protect those who were being taken advantage of. Righteous anger always begins with love for what is right, not hatred for people. Even in His intensity, Jesus remained fully in command. He did not harm anyone. He did not act rashly. Every movement was deliberate. This was not a loss of temper - it was a demonstration of authority. True godly anger is never reckless. It is strong, purposeful, and restrained. If our anger is selfish, unfocused, or uncontrolled, it is no longer righteous. Jesus shows us that holiness can be bold without being cruel, and truth can be forceful without being sinful.

This moment teaches us that not all anger is wrong. There is a kind of anger that reflects God's heart - anger that stands against injustice, defends holiness, and refuses to tolerate exploitation or hypocrisy. That is the anger that cleanses, not destroys. The Lord's actions were ignited by the misuse of the temple and the injustice taking place there. It bothered Jesus that the people were being exploited. The devout were being cheated and those especially vulnerable were the foreigners and the poor. This was not what the temple was for. The temple was called the "house of God" (Ezra 5:2) and this was the place where He would meet with His people. Is. 56:7 says,

"For My house shall be called a house of prayer for all nations." The house of God, the place where He dwells, is a holy place reserved for prayer and worship. Today He no longer dwells in a building but in the hearts of those who receive Jesus as their Savior.

1 Cor. 3:16 says, "Do you not know that you are God's temple and that God's Spirit dwells in you?" Heb. 3:6 says, "And we are God's house if we keep the courage and remain confident in our hope in Christ." You are now God's house of prayer. The ancient temple in Jerusalem is gone but your relationship with God remains strong. All the King's men know that prayer is a significant part of that relationship. All those who have entered into a relationship with God are to be people of prayer. God delights in having fellowship with His children, so much so that prayer is the lifeblood of the Christian faith. Prayer should not be a burden to you but a time of pure delight. Your passion for God makes you crave for those times when you can be alone with Him talking one-on-one. Prayer is not hard but is easy and enjoyable. You need to value prayer for this is how you bring God into every situation you face in life. Prayer is so important you need to pray at all times.

1 Thess. 5:16-18 says, "Rejoice always, pray without ceasing, in everything give thanks for this is the will of God in Christ Jesus for you." Charles Spurgeon said, "Prayer gives a channel to the pent-up sorrow of the soul, they flow away, and in their stead streams of sacred delight pour into your heart. When joy and prayer are married, their first child is gratitude." What Paul is saying is you need to pray continually. David, a man

after God's own heart, prayed without ceasing. He said in Ps. 55:17, "Evening and morning and at noon I will pray, and cry aloud, and He shall hear my voice." To begin, continue, and to end the day with God in prayer is supreme wisdom. Day and night David saw his enemies busy (vs. 10) and would meet their activity with continuous prayer. Bathe everything in life that concerns you in prayer. Jesus said in Matt. 7:7, "Ask, and it will be given to you; seek and you will find; knock and it will be opened to you." Notice that Paul first tells you to rejoice always. How can you do that?

He gives the answer by telling you to pray without ceasing. The more you pray, the more rejoicing you will do. Rejoicing stops being a reaction and becomes a lifestyle. Prayer aligns your heart with heaven, and heaven is full of joy. Prayer is not merely a duty you fulfill; it is a doorway you walk through. Every time you pray, you step out of the noise of the world and into the presence of God. And in that presence, something quiet but powerful happens - your heart begins to rejoice. Prayer sharpens spiritual vision. What once looked overwhelming begins to look manageable. What once felt hopeless starts to glow with promise. As you lay your burdens before God, He does not always remove them instantly, but He does replace heaviness with peace, confusion with clarity, and fear with confidence. Rejoicing is the natural response of a heart that realizes it is not alone. The more you pray, the more you trust. Prayer builds intimacy, and intimacy produces assurance.

When you talk with God consistently, you begin to recognize His faithfulness. You remember answered prayers, unexpected provisions, and quiet moments where strength came from nowhere but Him. Prayer is a vital part of a man's role as one of the King's men. You grow and prevail and become strong and mighty through your private time of fellowship with God. Prayer is the atmosphere in which you exist. This is why prayer must be your first response to anything and everything that comes your way and not your last resort. Col. 4:2 (NLT) says, "Devote yourselves to prayer with an alert mind and a thankful heart." The Message Bible says, "Pray diligently. Stay alert with your eyes wide open in gratitude." The Greek word for "devote" is "proskartereo" and it describes a steadfast single-minded fidelity to a certain course of action; to persist with intense effort. One who is devoted is caring, committed, concerned, dedicated, loyal, steadfast, and true.

Devotion implies a strong attachment, allegiance, and affection to someone or something. Do these words describe your prayer life? It should because your devotion to prayer will affect everything in your life. It is abundantly clear that God's will is that you pray continually. Being devoted means you are not forgetful of the great privilege you've been given to be able to go boldly to the throne of grace to find help in time of need (Heb. 4:16). When you're devoted you do whatever it takes to ensure that prayer with thanksgiving is a central part of your spiritual life. You need to talk to God moment by moment, hour by hour. Unceasing prayer is not restricted to a set time, place, or posture of ones body. It's about maintaining a constant attitude of being in God's presence during every waking moment of your day. This means you can pray anytime, anywhere. This shows you are forever conscious of your dependence on God for prayer is the gate through which He enters your circumstances.

Jesus prayed often and so should you. If anyone ever lived a life fully empowered by God, it was Jesus. Yet again and again in the Gospels, we find Him withdrawing to pray. This truth alone should stop us in our tracks. Jesus was the Son of God - perfect in wisdom, power, and authority - and still He prayed often. The Bible shows us that prayer was not an occasional habit for Jesus; it was a daily discipline and so it should be with you also. If you're not sure what to say when you pray, rest assured, the Lord will teach you. In fact, even the disciples asked Jesus to teach them. Luke 11:1 says, "One day Jesus was praying in a certain place. When He finished, one of His disciples said to Him, 'Lord, teach us to pray, as John also taught his disciples.'" Surprisingly, this is the only time in the four gospels where someone asked Jesus for a specific teaching. Watching Jesus, they saw how vital prayer is to the success of any ministry. Prayer was not a last resort - it was His first response.

Notice that the disciple did not ask for a repetitive prayer that they could repeat over and over again in a ritualistic manner, for a prayer prayed from memory and not the heart. In fact, Jesus warned against this type of prayer in Matt. 6:7. He said, "But when you pray, do not use vain repetitions as the heathen do." All they were doing was making noise. There was no passion in their prayers as they kept praying the same thing over and over again. Jesus said, "For they think that they will be heard for their many words" (vs. 7). Charles Spurgeon said some people pray as "a mere exercise of memory and it is absurd to imagine that such a parrot exercise can be pleasing to the living God." The disciple said "teach us to pray" not "teach us a prayer." Notice also that Jesus was not asked to teach them how to pray. The request was to "teach us to pray like You pray." Jesus response to this request is what is known as the "Lord's Prayer."

Jesus never said to recite this prayer over and over again. What He said in Matt. 6:7 was, "In this manner, therefore, pray." There is no record of believers using this prayer in any of the other prayer passages in the Bible. The Lord's Prayer is not a prayer but an outline for prayer, a model to follow when talking to God. This outline for prayer is very simple and very brief. When Jesus prayed He covered several different topics and He tells us what those are. It's His pattern on how we should pray. Jesus begins His teaching on prayer by telling us how to address God when we pray. We begin by saying, "Our Father in heaven" (Matt. 6:9). He is saying you need to connect with God relationally. God wants a relationship with you, so much so that He wants you to call Him "Father." He doesn't want to be viewed as some divine entity off in the cosmos somewhere. Jesus said the first word we must speak when we pray is "Father." Unless you can call Him "Father" from the heart and mean it, anything else you say will have no substance.

For sure, the word "Father" is the most important word we utter when talking to God. If you don't learn to say "Father" then you don't know His authority and have no intimate connection with Him. Rom. 8:15 says, "So you have not received a spirit that makes you fearful slaves. Instead, you received God's Spirit when He adopted you as His own children. Now we call Him, 'Abba, Father.'" The word "Abba" is an Aramaic word and is used as a term of endearment and intimacy, similar to the words "daddy" and "papa" used in modern languages. "Abba" is a term of warmth and sentiment on one hand and obedience on the other. All children are to be intimate with their father all the while knowing he has authority that commands obedience. Jesus prayed in the Garden of Gethsemane, "Abba, Father, all things are possible for You. Take this cup away from Me; nevertheless, not what I will, but what You will" (Matt. 14:16). Jesus was connecting emotionally and intimately with the Father but was also expressing His submission to Him.

The next thing we are taught to say is "Hallowed be Your name" (vs. 9). To hallow God's name means to honor it as holy, set apart, unmatched, and worthy of our deepest reverence. It is a declaration that God is not common, casual, or ordinary. He is sacred, glorious, and supreme above all else. In a world that often treats sacred things lightly, this prayer calls us back to reverence. It reminds us that before we ask God for daily bread, guidance, or deliverance, we first acknowledge who He is. Worship comes before requests. Honor comes before answers. God's name, character, and reputation must be set apart as being holy in this world in which we live. Webster's Dictionary says to be holy means "to be exalted or worthy of complete devotion as one perfect in goodness and righteousness." What a perfect description of our Father God. Jesus is saying that God's name should be the most valued thing in all the world.

To "hallow" something is to make it holy and to separate it and sanctify it.

Jesus is teaching us to say, "Father, may Your person, Your identity, Your character, Your reputation, Your very being always be honored. Hallowed be Your name." Always approach God with holy reverence, awe, and respect. Martin Luther said God's name is made holy and hallowed among us "when both our doctrine and our living are truly Christian." All believers everywhere should want the name of God to be hallowed. In heaven angelic creatures cry out, "Holy, holy, holy is the Lord of hosts; The whole world is full of His glory!" (Is. 6:3). God's name is to be honored and adored continually. Rev. 5:13 says, "To Him who sits on the throne and to the Lamb be blessing and honor and glory and power forever and ever!" When we say to the Father "hallowed be Thy name" we are saying we want His holy name to be worshipped, exalted, honored, and adored on earth as it is in heaven. Charles Spurgeon said, "May all men honor, reverence, and adore Thy holy name." This is what Jesus is telling us to do.

After praising and worshipping His holy name you move on to the next point on the outline and say, "Your kingdom come. Your will be done, on earth as it is in heaven" (vs. 10). Notice that the word "Your" is used twice in this verse. In any relationship that matters to you, you always focus on the other person's agenda first. You put their plan above your plan. Relationships flourishe when surrender replaces selfishness. Trust deepens when you honor another's purpose as worthy of your attention. When you place someone else's plan above your own, you communicate value. You say, "You matter to me." Unity grows when agendas bow to understanding. Jesus is saying when you pray to put God's agenda first. Pray for God's plan and will to be done on the earth and in your own personal life and not your own plan. When you pray "Thy kingdom come" you willingly relinquish the rule of your own life. You give up governing your daily affairs in order to let God decide what it is you should do.

This is so important that in Greek there is heavy emphasis on the words "come" and "be done." Jesus is saying to go before God and boldly say, "Come Thy kingdom! Be done Thy will!" After giving top priority to the things of God and what He wants, you are then encouraged by Jesus to pray for the things you need. Say to Him, "Give us this day our daily bread" (vs. 11). Saying this is a reflection of your continual need for His spiritual and physical sustenance. Daily you are to depend on Him for "all things that pertain to life and godliness" (2 Peter 1:3). Take comfort knowing that God will always give you all you need for day to day living if you will make the kingdom of God and His righteousness your primary concern (Matt. 6:33). Ps. 121:1,2 (TPT), "I look up to the mountains on hills, longing for God's help. But then I realize that our true help and protection is only from the Lord, our Creator who made the heavens and the earth." You don't need weekly bread or monthly bread or yearly bread. No, you need daily bread. No person can live a single day unless God sustains them every moment of every day.

Jesus knew that light and darkness don't mix so it was imperative that He include vs. 12 in His outline, "And forgive us our sins as we forgive those who sin against us." Just as real as the need for daily bread is the need for daily forgiveness. One nourishes the flesh; the other restores the heart. One keeps us alive physically; the other keeps us free spiritually. Andrew Murray said, "As bread is the first need of the body, so is forgiveness for the soul." God never intended forgiveness to be a one-time experience. He designed it to be daily just like bread. Bread sustains the body; forgiveness sustains the soul. This verse shows clearly that God's forgiveness flows to those who forgive. Be forewarned that unforgiveness shuts off the flow of forgiveness from the Father (Matt. 6:14,15). Jesus paid the price for all your sins on the cross but that doesn't give us the right to keep on sinning. God forbid. Just be aware that sin always creates a break in fellowship with the Father.

Once you're saved you become the righteousness of God in Christ Jesus (2 Cor. 5:21). Sin does not affect your eternal standing before God but it does effect your present relationship with Him. Hab. 1:13 says, "Your eyes are too pure to approve evil, and You cannot look on wickedness with favor." David's prayer of repentance in Ps. 51 illustrates this principle. He cried out in vs. 12, "Restore to me the joy of Your salvation." He did not ask for his salvation to be restored, but for his relationship with God to be restored so his joy could return. Jesus is saying to get your heart right with God and people. As you pray, ask the Father to search your heart and reveal to you anything and everything that is not pleasing to Him (Ps. 139:23,24). Forgiveness is the greatest need of the human heart.

1 John 1:9 says, "If we confess our sins, he is faithful and just to forgive us our sins and to cleanse us from all unrighteousness." As you forgive you can now be forgiven and live without being paralyzed by guilt and shame.

In closing, Jesus said, "And do not lead us into temptation, but deliver us from the evil one. For Yours is the kingdom and the power and the glory forever. Amen" (vs. 13). This is not a good translation because God does not lead anybody into temptation (James 1:13). The correct rendering of this verse is, "Do not allow us to be led into temptation." The enemy does not wait for perfect timing. He waits for tired hearts, distracted minds, wounded emotions, and unguarded moments. Daily you will be tempted to sin and you need God's help to not yield to it. The Passion Translation says, "Rescue us every time we face tribulation and set us free from evil." Temptation itself is not sin but yielding to it is. And the moment you begin relying on your own strength, you are already standing on unstable ground. John MacArthur said this prayer "is an appeal to God not to allow the inevitable tests and trials of life to become temptations that would prove overwhelming."

The basis for this request is God's promise in 1 Cor. 10:13 where The Passion Translation says, "God will be faithful to you. He will screen and filter the severity, nature, and timing of every test or trial you face so that you can bear it." Stand up and fight the devil in Jesus' name for His name is above every name (Phil. 2:9). Spiritual warfare is not something to avoid but to boldly enter into each and every day. Finally, Jesus tells you to end your time of prayer with where you began, by giving glory and honor to God. Tell the Father it's His kingdom, His power, and His glory forever. Amen. End every prayer by expressing your faith in God's ability. Jer. 32:17, "You have made the heavens and the earth by Your great power and outstretched arm. Nothing is too difficult for you." Finish praying with Rev. 5:13, "Blessing and honor and glory and power be to Him who sits on the throne, and to the Lamb, forever and ever!" Follow this outline and you will have prayed the perfect prayer.

# | 15 |

# "FAITH THAT WINS"

If you want to be successful in your walk with God, you'll have to learn how to walk by faith and not by sight (2 Cor. 5:7). Why is this so important? Because without faith it is impossible to please God (Heb. 11:6). In fact, faith is so important that Rom. 14:23 (AMP) says, "For whatever does not originate and proceed from faith is sin. Whatever is done without a conviction of its approval by God is sinful!" Faith is the willingness to put all of life before God for His approval. Charles Spurgeon said, "If you are not sure a thing is right, let it alone, for it will be sin to you." Commentator Leon Morris said, "Faith is basic to the whole Christian way of life. It is a humble reliance on God for salvation and for the living out of the implication of that salvation." Faith is absolutely essential in the life of every born again believer for it is one of the three foundations of the Christian life. 1 Cor. 13:13 says, "And now abide faith, hope, and love."

Eph. 2:8 says you can't be saved without faith, "For it is by grace you have been saved through faith, and this is not from yourselves, it is the gift of God." Understand that you don't get faith by saying over and over again, "I believe, I believe." Faith is the internal work of God in the heart of a person. Rom. 12:3 says, "God has dealt to each one a measure of faith." Nobody can say, "I would believe if only I had some faith." Everybody has a measure of faith. The question is, "Will you use the faith you've been given or won't you?" Faith gets stronger and increases when you act on the measure of faith you've been given. If you ignore the prompting of the Holy Spirit to act on faith, you'll lose what faith you do have. You must use it or lose it. Jesus said, "Whoever has will be given more, and they will have an abundance. Whoever does not have, even what they have will be taken from them" (Matt. 25:29).

You need to know that you can't receive anything from the Lord without faith. James 1:6,7 (TPT) says, "Just make sure you ask empowered by confident faith without doubting that you will receive. For the one who doubts is like a wave of the sea that is driven and tossed by the wind. For that person must not suppose that he will receive anything from the Lord." You can't see God intervene in your circumstances in a miraculous, supernatural way without faith. Matt. 13:58 says, "And He did not do many miracles there because of their lack of faith." On the other side of the coin, two blind men came to Jesus and Matt. 9:29,30 says, "Then He touched their eyes, saying, 'According to your faith be it done to you.' And their eyes were opened." Faith always starts in the invisible realm. It's "the substance of things hoped for, the evidence of things not seen" (Heb. 11:1). 2 Cor. 4:18, "So we fix our eyes not on what is seen, but on what is unseen. For what is seen is temporary, but what is unseen is eternal."

Everything you see is temporary. Your house, car, and job is all temporary. Even your problems are temporary. This world and everything in it will all pass away for it is only temporary. The question is, "Where are you looking?" How important it is that you continually look in the right direction. Elisha and his servant were surrounded by the enemy and the prophet looked into the unseen realm and said, "Don't be afraid, for those who are with us are more than those who are with them" (2 Kings 6:16). His servant couldn't see anything so Elisha prayed for his spiritual eyes to be opened. The result was "he looked and saw the hills full of horses and chariots of fire all around Elisha" (vs. 17). This is why we are called upon to walk by faith and not by sight. It is through faith that you see into the unseen realm. Faith sees the invisible and hears the inaudible.

How can things unseen and invisible be looked at? With eyes of faith that give you the ability to see beyond physical realities and limitations and focus on God's will and promises. To walk by faith you must forever be looking at what is unseen. The Greek word for "look" is "skopeo" and it means 'to spy out; to notice carefully; examine; pay attention to.' The essential idea here is to keep a watchful eye on something, being concerned about it and to contemplate it and keep thinking about it. It's when you regard something as being important. The things of this world are only temporary and are not to be the goal of a man's existence. All the King's men are to continually scope out the invisible things of eternity. Charles Spurgeon said, "The things which are seen are not worth looking at, so temporary are they, while the things unseen are of priceless worth, because they are eternal."

Always fix your eyes on the eternal. It's through faith that you can see the unseen. Anglican cleric Charles Simeon said, "To a man who has heaven in his eye, nothing is impossible. Faith is opposed to sight, and has respect entirely to things which are beyond the reach of mortal eyes. It looks upon an unseen God, it views an unseen Savior and views an unseen heaven also." Faith always starts in the invisible realm but it impacts the visible realm. Jesus said, "The Son can do nothing of Himself; He can only do what He sees the Father doing" (John 5:19). What Jesus saw in the invisible realm He carried out in the visible realm. This is how faith works. What you need is in the heavenly realm and faith brings it to the earthly realm. Open your spiritual eyes and see the rewards God has graciously bestowed upon you. With eyes of faith you can perceive all the blessings in the invisible realm that are yours for the taking.

Unfortunately, one of the most misunderstood verses in the Bible concerning faith is also one of the most popular. Rom. 10:17 says, "So then faith comes by hearing, and hearing by the word of God." It is often taught that faith comes by hearing yourself quote scriptures out loud. Yes, it's possible for faith to increase this way but this is not what this verse is saying. The Greek word "logos" is the written Word of God but the Greek word used here is "rhema." This word refers to    a specific word or revelation given to an individual at a particular moment. In other words, faith comes by hearing the voice of God. What happens when you read your Bible is that it sensitizes you to the will of God and to the voice of God. Reading your Bible tunes your life into hearing the voice of God and this is where faith originates. Yes, His voice can be heard through scripture but He'll also speak to you personally.

The Bible is full of stories of God speaking one-on-one with people. They heard His voice and they believed what He said. "Faith is birthed in a heart that responds to God's anointed utterance" (TPT). The angel Gabriel said to Mary in Luke 1:37, "For nothing will be impossible with God." The Greek translation says, "For nothing will be impossible with any rhema from God." A "rhema" word from God will tell you exactly how to respond to your specific circumstance. A "rhema" word can help you hear the voice of God in a new light so you can apply it to your life. An example of a "rhema" word was when Jesus told Peter to cast his nets on the other side of the boat. Peter heard the voice of Jesus, he responded accordingly, and caught an abundance of fish. Any word you get from God, whether it be a verse of scripture or something God says to you personally, when believed by faith and acted upon, will bring you supernatural results.

You need to know that the one thing the devil wants to attack most in your life is your faith. His attacks on your marriage and health and finances is in reality an attack on your faith. He's after your faith because it's faith that moves mountains, it's faith that saves marriages, it's faith that brings supernatural increase, it's faith that stirs heaven and rebukes hell. A good working definition of faith is that it is a gift from God that comes from hearing His voice and enables a person to believe God's Word and His will for their lives. Faith is more than speaking out what it is you believe. It must turn into action until it becomes not only a part of your life but a new way to live altogether. Faith comes when you hear the voice of God and respond to it. The essence of faith consists in believing and receiving what God has revealed and then acting on it.

Faith responds to the invisible. It hears the voice of God and, on the basis of that alone, on believing what you heard was true, you put action to your faith and do what God tells you to do. Through faith you understand in your spirit before your mind can comprehend it. If things have to make sense to you before you act on it, you'll never walk in faith. Heb. 11:3 (TPT), "Faith empowers us to see that the universe was created and beautifully coordinated by the power of God's words! He spoke and the invisible realm gave birth to all that is seen." Your spirit can easily comprehend the story of creation even though you can never understand it in your mind. This is how faith works. You understand it first in your heart and then in your head. It's in your heart that you hear the voice of God. It then becomes your responsibility to respond accordingly to what you hear Him saying. Do that and you'll be walking in faith.

Strong faith takes action and Heb. 11:7 says Noah was a man who took action, "By faith Noah was warned about things not yet seen, in holy fear built an ark to save his family." We learn from Noah that strong faith starts moving. Strong faith is a moving faith. It takes action. When God says to do something, you do it with no questions asked. Notice that Noah was warned about things not seen. God told him it was going to rain for 40 days and 40 nights. This played tricks with his mind because he had never seen rain before. Gen. 2:5,6 (NIV) says, "For the Lord God had not sent rain on the earth but streams came up from the earth and watered the whole surface of the ground." All during Noah'a life the ground was watered by the morning dew and it was mind-boggling to comprehend water falling from the sky. But he built the ark anyway.

He believed God and put action to his faith when the rest of the world thought he was a madman. Faith operates not in what you understand but on what the voice of God says to you. We also learn from Noah that strong faith takes a stand against evil. Heb. 11:7, "By his faith he condemned the world and became heir of the righteousness what is according to faith." What this means is that while he's building the ark he's publicly declaring the truth to a lost an dying world. 2 Peter 2:5 goes so far to call Noah "a preacher of righteousness." Noah was a light in a dark world and with every striking blow of his hammer he proclaimed that judgment was coming to a world of wicked people who had never experienced rain. He took a stand for righteousness not caring what others thought of him. You also need to take a stand. If you don't, Jesus said, "Whoever denies Me before men, him I will deny before My Father" (Matt. 10:33).

Faith is not a feeling. It's a substance. It's real and it's measurable. It's visible in the eyes of God. Mark 9:2 says, "When Jesus saw their faith..." Invisible faith is seen in visible actions. James

2:26 says, "So also faith without works is dead." Faith that wins always has a plan of action. Abraham offering his son Isaac on the altar was an action that proved the reality of his faith. All true believers have a faith that never stands around with its hands in its pockets. True faith, a faith that wins, produces a life full of actions and not a head full of facts. The clear sign of your faith is not what you say but what you do. Words are dirt cheap when they have not a plan of action attached to them. You must get out on a limb and put action to your faith. James 2:14 asks, "What does it profit, my brethren, if someone says he has faith but does not have works?" Vs. 24 then says, "You see that a man is justified by works and not by faith alone."

Faith is demonstrated by the works you do. Faith that does not result in action is ineffective and does not fulfill its intended purpose. For sure, faith without works is a dead faith. Hebrews 11 is full of stories of people who put action to their faith. Abel offered to God a more excellent sacrifice (vs. 4), Abraham left his home country (vs. 7), and Rahab welcomed the spies with peace (vs. 31). The list goes on and on. James 2:18 says, "But someone will say, 'You have faith, and I have works.' Show me your faith without your works, and I will show you my faith by my works." Commentator Adam Clarke said, "Your pretending to have faith while you have no works is utterly vain." God doesn't just want to hear what you believe, He also wants you to show Him by your actions. Faith and actions are two sides of the same coin and are always found together in the scriptures. Separate them and they  have no value at all. Together they're able to change your world.

It is through faith that all the battles of life are won. 1 John 5:4 (TPT) says, ""Every child of God overcomes the world, for our faith is the victorious power that triumphs over the world." If you want to be a man of faith, then you'll need a faith that wins. God wants all of us to be victors and not victims, to grow and soar and overcome, not to be overwhelmed. You fight the good fight of faith to overcome the world, the flesh, and the devil. 1 Cor. 15:57 says, "Thanks be to God who gives us the victory through our Lord Jesus Christ." Faith that wins conquers the world when we cling to eternal realities. Andrew Murray said, "Conformity to the world can be overcome by nothing but conformity to Jesus." He who is constantly conquering the world and gaining victory in all areas of life is the man whose faith is embraced in the confession that Jesus is the Christ, the Son of the living God.

The Greek word for "overcome" is "nikao" and it means 'to conquer; to be victorious; to prevail in the face of obstacles.' It's when you go onward and upward in the power of a faith that wins. The word "faith" is the celebration of victory. It produces joy unspeakable. It brings confidence and it gives hope. It produces the blessed life. It's the victory that overcomes the world. Faith gives you the victory in your personal life, your professional life, and in your spiritual life. It gives you victory over sickness and disease and over fear and insecurity. Faith gives you victory over habits and emotions that enslave you. It gives you victory over your troubled past and gives you a bright future that is filled with God's sunshine and love. Rev. 2 and 3 tells of the many special blessings to those who overcome. Every good thing that God offers to His people come to you on the wings of faith which is the currency of heaven.

Faith that wins touches the invisible and laughs at the impossible. It commands mountains of spiritual barriers to be removed and they are cast into the sea and removed forevermore. Faith stands in God's mighty power and is robed in His glorious majesty. It wears royal apparel and rides on the King's horse. Nothing shall be impossible to the man who walks by faith. Faith goes farther than what the eye can see. Faith is not believing God can do something, it's believing He will do it even when your circumstances are contrary to what you're believing for. A lot people can believe God about everything except for help in the midst of their current trial. This should not be for when your heart is right with God, faith takes no effort at all. We walk by faith and not by sight. If you don't believe it, you'll never see it. Once you believe that nothing is impossible with God, you've crossed over from the natural to the supernatural.

Jesus said in Mark 9:23, "If you can believe, all things are possible to him that believes." Yes, God is all powerful but Charles Spurgeon said, "Our unbelief ties the hands of His omnipotence." He also said, "We can bear our load of trouble, or pass uninjured through the waves of distress, if we can gird our loins with the girdle of peace which is buckled on by the hands of trust. It is not right that thou should grovel in the dust, O child of a King. Ascend! The golden throne of assurance is waiting for you. The crown of communion with Jesus is ready to decorate your brow. Wrap yourself in scarlet and fine linen for if thou believeth, thy land shall flow with milk and honey and thy soul shall be satisfied as with marrow and fatness. Gather golden sheaves of grace, for they await thee in the fields of faith. All things are possible to him that believeth." The benefits of walking by faith cannot be better expressed.

# | 16 |

# "FINISH STRONG"

We've all heard the old saying, "It's not how you start that matters, it's how you finish." All of God's children finish strong their journey in life because they know their Savior did the same thing. The Lord said in Zech. 8:9 (NLT), "Be strong and finish the task." When He walked the earth He said, "My food is to do the will of Him who sent Me and to finish His work" (John 4:34). He knew His assignment would lead to the cross but He pressed on anyway. He fulfilled what He came to do and with His last breath He cried out, "It is finished!" He finished strong and so will you. William Barclay said, "Jesus died with a shout of triumph on His lips. He did not say 'It is finished!' in weary defeat; He said it as one who shouts for joy because the victory was won." Jesus died with a war cry of victory. Three days later He would miraculously arise from the dead having defeated death, hell, and the grave. He finished strong and changed humanity forevermore.

Live your life in such a way that when all is said and done you'll end your journey with an exclamation mark! People of

God never burn out and as each year passes they get stronger and stronger. They fight to the bitter end with the words Jesus spoke in Luke 9:62 burned on their heart, "No one, after putting his hand to the plow and looking back, is fit for the kingdom of God." The Passion Translation says, "Why do you keep looking back to your past and have second thoughts about following Me? If you turn back you are not fit for God's kingdom." Paul said in 2 Tim. 4:7, "I have fought the good fight, I have finished the race, I have kept the faith." The whole point of a race is that it has a finish line. You must always finish what you begin. Winston Churchill is famous for saying, "Never give in, never give in; never; never; never - in nothing great or small, large or petty - never give in except to conviction of honor and good sense."

Real men and women of God never turn back but keep moving forward with force and perseverance. They "press toward the mark for the prize of the high calling of God in Christ Jesus" (Phil. 3:14). To finish strong you must run your race with passion and purpose. Never lose sight of your heavenly calling as you let go of anything and everything that tries to hold you back. Embrace Jesus as your Lord and Savior. Be consumed with your love for Him and long to experience His resurrection power in your life each and every day. Forget the past and look to the finish line of your life. Dig your heels in and run your race with all your heart, soul, and might. Let nothing stop you from fulfilling your destiny. Every life has a beginning and an end. You had no say-so in getting born but you have everything to say about how your life will end. Run at a pace that allows you to finish strong.

An anonymous poet once wrote, "You cannot go back and make a brand new start my friend, but anyone can start now and make a brand new end." Amen to that! Always remember that a quitter never wins and a winner never quits. Even if the odds are stretched against you, be determined to never throw in the towel and never surrender. Unfortunately, we live in a world where quitting is expected. How sad it is that "no fault" divorces are happening each and every day. People today need grit. Either win or die trying. Yes, obstacles are a part of life. It's what you do with them that either strengthens or weakens your character. When you face obstacles head on, you'll be a better person because of it. It doesn't matter how old or young you are, finishing strong must become the goal of every child of God. Eccl. 7:8 says, "The end of a matter is better than its beginning."

Real men and women love to win and this is why they never quit and always finish strong. Winning the battle between good and evil should be your motivation when you wake up each morning. Face each day with guts and determination. Never, never give up. Prov. 24:16 says, "For a righteous man may fall seven times and rise again." That is the mark of a true winner. It is the will of God that any divine assignment you undertake be finished. Fight to the bitter end and never quit. Finishing strong should be the top priority of your life. To finish strong you must forget the past and press on to what lies ahead. Follow the calling God selected for you. Learn from your mistakes and become the person God created you to be. Finish strong each and every day. Finish strong today and finish strong tomorrow. You're a believer, a strong believer.

You are a hero because you're a person who finishes each day strong.

To finish strong you must make a quality decision that you will indeed finish strong. Set goals to become the person the world needs you to be. Aim to finish well what you begin. Be like Paul who wanted to complete his journey of faith. He said in Acts 20:24, "But my life is worth nothing to me unless I use it for finishing the work assigned to me by the Lord Jesus." Paul knew he was not his own but that his life belonged to Jesus in whose hands he was a "chosen instrument" (Acts 9:15). What he's saying here is duty is more important than life itself. Paul patterned his life after the example of Jesus who completed His mission. He wouldn't let anything distract him from his goal of completing his journey and finishing it well. Nothing, absolutely nothing, would deter Paul from fulfilling his holy purpose. He said in Phil. 1:21, "For to me, to live is Christ and to die is gain." No wonder he finished strong.

Like Paul, you've got one life to live and one race to run. Take possession of the truth that you were put on this earth to run your own race and not someone else's race. Heb. 12:1 says, "Let us run with endurance the race that is set before us." You are in a race and God has a lane for you to run in and a finish line for you to cross. Paul knew why he was here. He knew his assignment was to faithfully preach the wonderful news of God's grace. You also have an assignment specifically designed by God Himself. When you know what your calling is, do everything you can to finish strong in the fulfillment of it. Paul told Timothy, "Do the work of an evangelist, fulfill your ministry" (2 Tim. 4:5). To finish strong there must be active engagement on your part. With extreme effort you must put everything you've got into it even when it is difficult and requires sacrifice.

So committed was Paul to finish strong that he said in Acts 21:13, "For I am ready not only to be imprisoned but even to die in Jerusalem for the name of the Lord Jesus." Finishing strong involves staying focused on God's goals and working hard to achieve them. Fulfilling your ministry requires faithfulness in the small things so you can be made ruler over the big things. You must count the cost of running your race and be willing to intentionally put forth continual diligence and effort. Paul said in 1 Cor. 9:24, "Run in such a way that you may win." This is not a suggestion; it is a command. Run your race with dedication and zeal. Go for the gold and finish strong. The goal of every race is to win. To do that you must lay aside all distractions. Paul said in 2 Tim. 2:4, "No man, acting as a soldier for God, entangles himself in worldly affairs, so that he may be pleasing to him who enlisted him as a soldier."

To finish strong you must recognize that God has entrusted a ministry to you. You are not here to putter around serving God in your spare time whenever you feel like it. There is no such thing as a child of God without a ministry. 1 Peter 4:10 says, "God has given each of us a gift from His great variety of spiritual gifts. Use them well to serve one another." Every man has received a supernatural talent and ability from God. At the end of time everybody will give an account to Him of his stewardship in using that gift for God's purposes (Matt.

25:14-30). This is why it is so important that you finish strong. You don't limp across the finish line but boldly and strongly cross over it by pouring all your heart and soul into the work you've been called to do. Like a blank check sign your life over to God allowing Him to use you according to His purposes. Go all out for Him knowing He'll give you the grace to finish strong in your endeavors.

Completing any race takes time, effort, and stamina. The longer the race, the more stamina will be required. You're in this for the long haul and you must push yourself every day. Put one foot in front of the other and keep the momentum going. Don't stop when you reach the summit of one mountain. Keep going and find a bigger and taller mountain to climb. Keep climbing and keep running until you reach the finish line. Keep taking things a notch higher with each step you take. Continually go onward and upward in your quest to fulfill your destiny. Grab hold of the assignment God has for you. Embrace the vision. Cling to the call on your life. God did not anoint you with His power so you could run away when the going gets tough. You're bigger than that! 2 Cor. 4:8 (TPT) says, "Though we experience every kind of pressure, we're not crushed. At times we don't know what to do, but quitting is not an option."

To finish strong you must always focus on the outcome of whatever it is you are trying to do. Joseph kept alive in his heart the dream God had given him that one day he would be in a position of authority. Before the fulfillment of this dream he was sold into slavery by his jealous brothers and later thrown into prison for shunning the lustful advances of

Potiphar's wife. Despite all that, Joseph was a champion of the highest order and he did not quit. He finished strong by becoming a wise leader who saved thousands of people when a seven-year drought ravaged the land. 1 Cor. 7:20 says, "Let each man abide in the same calling wherein he was called." To finish strong and fulfill the call on your life will take time, commitment, and a refusal to quit. We learn from Joseph that when things go wrong, when plans get interrupted, if you will put your trust in God there is always hope and assurance that your God-given dream will come to pass.

Your vision from God, when grabbed onto, will become your reason and purpose for living. Your future will be consumed by your desire to fulfill completely this high calling from God. You have an assignment from God so run with it. Set goals, plan ahead, and get to work with the intention of finishing strong. Be consistent for you will become what you do regularly and often. David was consistent. He killed the lion and the bear and then went on to kill Goliath. Trust God and keep going forward at all times. The worst thing you can do is sit back and do nothing. Great people are ordinary people with extraordinary amounts of determination. Rise up and never let lions and bears and giants keep you idle. Grab hold of the victory that is waiting for you. March forward and keep your head held high when trials come. Put you confidence in the words spoken in Nahum 1:3, "But the Lord has His way in the whirlwind and in the storm."

To finish strong you must have great endurance. Some parts of your journey will be easy but other times they will be very challenging to the point where you'll be tempted to give up. It takes time and effort for most things to come to fruition. For this reason Heb. 10:36 says, "For you have need of endurance so that after you have done the will of God you may receive the promise." The writer of Hebrews is issuing a call for perseverance and persistence, needed traits in the Christian journey. We live in an ungodly world full of hardship and adversity and endurance is essential. Endurance refers to being durable under pressure. Life is like a long marathon race and you must be able to withstand hardship and adversity over a prolonged period of time. Jesus emphasized the need for endurance when He said in Matt. 10:22, "You will be hated by everyone because of Me, but the one who stands firm to the end will be saved."

The Greek word "hupomone" portrays a picture of unflinchingly bearing up under a heavy load that doesn't allow one to surrender to circumstances or succumb under trial. You will finish strong when you stand firm to the end. You are to live a life of constancy and endurance with a forward look and the ability to focus on what is beyond your current trial. You can do it if you'll learn from Jesus "who for the joy that was set before Him endured the cross, despising the shame, and has sat down at the right hand of the throne of God" (Heb. 12:2). He assessed what He was going through in the light of eternity (2 Cor. 4;16-18). He focused on the reward on the other side of the cross and this gave Him the ability to withstand what He went through. James 1:12 says, "Blessed is the man who remains steadfast under trial, for when he has stood the test he will receive the crown of life which God has promised to those who love Him."

Patient endurance is what you need so that you will continue to do the will of God. Deliverance from all your problems is not what you need, endurance is what you need. God will give you the power to endure hardship and people will be drawn to Christ when they see this power at work in you. They couldn't see this power if all your problems were taken away. God wants you to endure trials with blazing hope knowing that doing so leads to glory. This is not patience that grimly waits for the end, it is patience that radically hopes for a new dawn. With endurance your trial will lead you to a strong finish. The one who wins the prize is the one who endures to the end, the one who hears the Lord say, "Well done, good and faithful servant" (Matt. 25:21). Strong believers triumphantly face difficult circumstances knowing that even out of evil God guarantees good. They accept suffering and hardship and turn them into grace and glory.

Andrew Murray said, "Without perseverance, endurance, and steadfastness faith is vain. The only proof it is a living, strong faith is that it holds its boldness firm to the end." Trust God and He will be the source of your endurance. 1 Thess. 1:3 says, "We remember before our God and Father your endurance inspired by hope in our Lord Jesus Christ." God is faithful. He is the God of all impossibilities. He is the Lord of the Breakthrough. David said in 2 Sam. 5:20, "The Lord has broken through my enemies before me, like a breakthrough of waters." Keep hope alive knowing that "He who has begun a good work in you will complete it until the day of Jesus Christ" (Phil. 1:6). God reassured Zerubbable that He would complete what He started in him. The Lord said in Zech. 4:9, "The hands of

Zerubbable have laid the foundation of this temple; His hands shall also finish it. Then you will know that the Lord of hosts has sent Me to you."

There is a promise for every season of life you go through. Your heart will leap inside you when you realize that when you endure "you will receive all that He has promised" (Heb. 10:36). God is the great promise keeper, and He will make good on His promise to reward you when you remain faithful to the call on your life, when you endure to the end, and when you finish strong. Col. 3:23,24 says, "And whatever you do, do it heartily, as to the Lord and not to men, knowing that from the Lord you will receive the reward of the inheritance, for you serve the Lord." Whatever you do should be done with all your might (Eccl. 9:10), in the name of the Lord Jesus (Col. 3:17), to the glory of God (1 Cor. 10:31). Do everything with enthusiasm, confidence, and diligence. Let there be "glory in the grind." Let your labor of love be done with dignity knowing it is the Lord you serve. This should motivate you to always do your best in whatever you do.

It is the duty of all believers to work for the glory of God. Make it your task to make your labor a testimony to God's glory knowing that no service to Him goes unnoticed. Matt. 6:3,4 (TPT), "But when you demonstrate generosity, do it with pure motives and without drawing attention to yourselves. Give secretly and your Father, who sees all you do, will reward you openly." When you perform acts of kindness and generosity without seeking recognition or praise, God will acknowledge   and reward your works of service in a visible and public way. Notice the emphasis that it is God Himself who will reward you, and what a great reward it will be. Any praise from His lips and any reward from His hands will be of priceless value. Rev. 22:12 says, "And behold, I am coming quickly, and My reward is with Me, to give to everyone according to his work." This is what awaits those who finish strong.

# SUMMARY

As we reach the end of this journey, one truth stands clear: God has called you to be more than ordinary. You are an ambassador, a warrior, a vessel of honor in His Kingdom. The principles in this book are not merely ideas - they are a blueprint for living a life of faith, courage, and authority in Christ.

You have learned to pray boldly, to walk in godly character, and to exercise the authority God has entrusted to you. You have been reminded that every battle is winnable, every challenge conquerable, and every circumstance an opportunity to demonstrate the power of the Kingdom through your life.

But knowledge alone is not enough. What matters is action. Stand firm. Run your race with determination. Finish strong. Reflect Christ in everything you do, influence those around you, and leave a lasting legacy for generations to come.

The call of the King is still before you. The world is waiting to see the light of His Kingdom shine through men who are fully surrendered, fully committed, and fully alive in their purpose. Go forth with boldness, courage, and unwavering faith because as one of "All The King's Men," you are empowered to change the world, one life at a time.